DREAMS FROM GOD

A Glimpse of the Future by God's Grace

Susan C. McDermott

Illustrations by: Sonny Heston

authorHOUSE®

AuthorHouse™
1663 Liberty Drive
Bloomington, IN 47403
www.authorhouse.com
Phone: 1 (800) 839-8640

This book is a work of non-fiction. Unless otherwise noted, the author and the publisher make no explicit guarantees as to the accuracy of the information contained in this book and in some cases, names of people and places have been altered to protect their privacy.

Published by AuthorHouse   02/10/2016

ISBN: 978-1-5049-6429-6 (sc)
ISBN: 978-1-5049-6428-9 (e)

Library of Congress Control Number: 2015919673

Print information available on the last page.

Any people depicted in stock imagery provided by Thinkstock are models, and such images are being used for illustrative purposes only. Certain stock imagery © Thinkstock.

This book is printed on acid-free paper.

Back Cover Photo

The photo is of Grossglockner at sunrise. Grossglockner is the highest peak in the Austrian Alps. This photo was taken over sixty years ago by a relative of my father.

To my sons, David and Michael Cummings, for being the most important part of my life. I am so proud of you both. You have grown into wonderful men and loving fathers.

To my loving husband, John, my best friend and helpmate who loves me for who I am.

To David's wife, Jamie, for being a wonderful daughter-in-law and for raising two great boys.

To Michael's girlfriend, Jessica, for being sweet and for loving my son and granddaughters.

To our daughter, Shannon, a wonderful and loving daughter.

To my wonderful grandmother, Frieda Caroline Lemke, my second mother who taught me useful skills.

To my father, Helmuth A. Sporbeck, my inspiration in tough times, for his unwavering fatherly love.

To my mother, Ilse E. L. Sporbeck, who taught me and molded me into who I am.

To Michael's and David's children, Karis, Kaia, Kyle and Ian. G-McD loves you.

CONTENTS

PREFACE

*For My thoughts are not your thoughts, nor are your ways
My ways, says the LORD. For as the heavens are higher than
the earth, so are My ways higher than your ways, and My
thoughts than your thoughts.* (Isaiah 55:8–9 NKJV)

There is something mysterious about the way God works. Through
His means of grace, He enters your life at a moment's notice through
a thought, a dream, or an audible voice. Peace, joy, and love are the
outpourings of the Holy Spirit that give you the very limited knowledge
that something spiritual and holy has occurred. Surprise, amazement,
and wonder seem to follow. I know it did for me.

We know God only so far as He enters into relationship with us
to accomplish His will for us. R. A. Torrey said it best in his book *The
Person and Work of The Holy Spirit*, "The Holy Spirit is not a power that
we get hold of and use according to our will but a Person of sovereign
majesty, who uses us according to His will." The Holy Spirit reveals
Himself to us in the Holy Scriptures. In Acts 2:16–21 Peter addresses
the crowd saying,

> No, this is what was spoken by the prophet Joel
>> In the last days, God says,
>> I will pour out my spirit on all people.
>> Your sons and daughters will prophesy.
>> Your young men will see visions,

your old men will dream dreams.
Even on my servants, both men and women,
I will pour out my spirit in those days,
and they will prophesy.
I will show wonders in the heaven above
and signs on the earth below,
blood and fire and billows of smoke.
The sun will be turned to darkness
and the moon to blood
before the coming of the great and
glorious day of the Lord.
And everyone who calls on the
name of the Lord will be saved.

What to do with the knowledge imparted to you is the question. You were given no instruction manual to follow or to help you. You ponder in utter amazement upon the gift given you, searching first why you were picked to be blessed. Now you must choose how to handle the gift.

I don't remember praying for God to enter my life in such a dramatic way, yet He did. I have been enormously blessed through my encounter with the living God.

Where do you begin an amazing and wonderful story? Maybe briefly at the beginning. But the unfolding of this story takes a lifetime.

Acknowledgments

A very special thank you to my friend Joan K. Hyer, Waterloo, Wisconsin, for all her help with editing and her encouragement. Joan and her husband, Jim, were wonderful friends and neighbors. They lived next to our farm in the old school house.

Thank you to Pastor James Adomeit, St. John Evangelical Lutheran Church (WELS), Waterloo, Wisconsin, for reviewing the manuscript and his helpful suggestions.

Thank you to Alida Rompelman and Elsbeth Fuchs for their joy and support. They both live on farms near Waterloo, Wisconsin.

Thank you to David and Naomi Plocher for their encouragement.

PART 1

A Simple Lifestyle

CHAPTER 1

My Inspirations

Let me give you a brief background of my family. I lived with my maternal grandmother, who emigrated from Germany before World War II with my grandfather and mother and settled in Milwaukee, Wisconsin. My grandmother was a quiet but strong woman. Imagine bringing your family to a new land, not speaking the language, having to find a place to live and get a job, and then going through the Great Depression.

My grandparents had one daughter, my mother. My mother never really talked about her childhood, except to say that her father never hugged her or told her he loved her. But my grandmother was loving even in the midst of trying to cope with all the challenges of a new country. My grandfather eventually divorced my grandmother and left for parts unknown, leaving my grandmother to care for my mother and try to make a living. My grandfather was an uncaring, very selfish person. I don't ever remember meeting him.

My grandmother found work stripping tobacco, which was a miserable job. In her later years, she cared for wealthy children when their parents were away on business or pleasure. I had the utmost admiration for my grandmother. In a way, she became my mother and taught me how to sew, bake, and make soap, but most of all to be frugal. I lived with her until I graduated from high school.

My father's family (left to right): My father's brother
Karl, great-grandmother, Grandmother Elizabeth, my
father Helmuth A., and Grandfather Karl Sporbeck.

My father was my other inspiration. He also emigrated from Germany with his family when he was young and settled in Milwaukee, Wisconsin. My dad was an accomplished musician and was first chair violinist in Germany. German schools were very different from American schools. They were extremely disciplined. If the lines going in from recess were not perfectly straight, whoever was out of line received a hard slap.

My father started school in the United States around the age of ten. This was a challenge because he spoke no English. A few years after coming to America, his father passed away, leaving my father, his older and younger brothers, and his mother. This had to be extremely hard on my grandmother. My memories of my paternal grandmother were not very loving or happy. She was a stern woman who never smiled or did anything with my sister or me. She lived with her youngest son.

At the beginning of the Depression, my father had just finished the eighth grade. His mother decided to send him to live with his grandfather, whom he had never met and who lived in a cabin in Northern California, where he worked as a logger. My father was to work with him and send money back to support the family. Why the older brother was not sent, my father never said. I assumed the older brother was his mom's favorite.

California was almost two thousand miles away from their home in Wisconsin. My father left with his grandfather, taking the train to California. His grandfather was a thoughtless person; he let my father sit on a hard bench in the smoking car and not tell him he could sit in the passenger car. I can't imagine being that young and traveling with someone who was not loving or caring.

My father, a thoughtful and caring person, had to live in a dirty, filthy cabin in the woods of Northern California with a man who didn't care; it must have been awful and depressing. My father was a perfectionist and very neat. Having to live with a dirty man who smoked cigars and couldn't cook was a living hell. But being the wonderful man my father was, even at fourteen years of age, he worked hard and sent his money home.

Photo taken at Mirror Lake in Yosemite National Park, California (left to right): My great-grandfather, my father, my grandmother Elizabeth, and my father's brother Hans.

Today, if children don't have a smartphone, tablet, and Facebook page they consider life a hell.

After a few years, my father found a job working for a wealthy family taking care of their property. He lived in a small room with all of his things and pack rats for company, who always carried off his things, but this place was ten times better than living with his grandfather.

My father learned to cook and hunt for food and took classes and educated himself. He finally moved back to Milwaukee, Wisconsin, after the Depression.

CHAPTER 2

My Beginning

My childhood was normal. I had two loving parents, and my maternal grandmother lived with us in Milwaukee, Wisconsin.

My family
(Left to right) My grandmother Frieda Lemke,
mother Ilse, and father Helmuth.

I went to school and enjoyed summer vacations. I have one sister who is four years younger than me. Our family was small, having only two uncles, two aunts, and two cousins. My parents were loving but strict perfectionists. My sister and I grew up knowing where our boundaries were and what was expected of us.

As a child, I was taken to church by my parents. I had a basic Christian upbringing in a conservative branch of the Lutheran church. Most times I did not understand anything that was taught, but I was still hearing the Word of God. I always enjoyed being at church.

When I was thirteen, I was moved upstairs to live with my grandmother. She had the top half of our duplex. I enjoyed living with her, but it also distanced me from my family. It was very lonely, as my grandmother would be gone for several weeks taking care of other children.

I loved going to school and participating in everything. I excelled in my studies and joined many clubs, including German club, dance ensemble, and drill team. Sports and gym class were not my strong suits. Actually, I should have flunked gym class.

During this time, I always felt drawn to church. Was church my sanctuary? Singing in the choir and youth group gatherings seemed to fill a void and bring me fun and happiness. I was shy and naive and never dated in high school.

After high school, I went off to college and lived at the school. My grandmother passed away the summer I graduated from high school. I truly missed her warmth and love.

Susan C. McDermott

During college, with studies taking up a lot of time, church seemed distant and I often didn't go. I was studying to be a home economics teacher, with a secret minor in art and chemistry. I could sew really well, and that was about it. I really wanted to be a commercial artist. But since my parents were paying for college, I enrolled in home economics. I tried going to church but never found the right one. Needless to say, since I was busy with school and working part-time, church became absent in my life.

CHAPTER 3

Marriage and Divorce

After graduation from college in 1969, I was married. My husband and I lived on a small farm near the town of Waterloo, Wisconsin. Waterloo is a small farm town with four corners as the center of town. However, it is a busy town for only having thirty-five hundred residents. Most of the people in the town were born and raised there. They were welcoming and friendly, and I felt right at home. Coming from a large city like Milwaukee, living in a small town should have been a shock, but it wasn't. Everyone seem to know everyone, and I liked that sense of community. I felt at home.

We were married quite a few years before we had children. We decided on two kids, even though I secretly wanted to have a large family. Two wonderful boys kept me busy from dawn to dusk.

(left to right)
My sons, Michael and David.

My husband was the only man I ever dated. Remember, I was very shy and naive and had a hard time talking to men. I was unsure about myself. In my heart, I knew I shouldn't marry him, and I think he knew it. But we married anyway.

We then divorced when the boys were small. Divorce is never the correct answer, but it seemed okay to me at the time. I hoped my ex-husband would find someone who was more compatible with him than I, and I was expecting to find someone who would love me for myself and who had the same ideas and goals.

My parents had a wonderful marriage. They were best friends, enjoyed each other, and did everything together. I secretly hoped and prayed there was someone out there for me who would be my best friend and husband. That hope kept me going. I hated being without a husband, but that was the decision I made.

Now I needed church, a sense of belonging, and a purpose. Life was not easy as a single mother with no job. I had very little money coming in—only $400 a month and that had to cover all expenses, such as rent, electricity, fuel oil for heating, gas for the car, and car maintenance. There was very little left over for food and clothes, and the entertainment budget was nonexistent. But looking back on that time, I see that I became more mature and much stronger.

My grandmother and dad were the best inspirations a child could have. No matter how bad your life is, if you work hard and do not give up, anything is possible. My life seemed wonderful compared to theirs, so I was not about to feel sorry for myself.

CHAPTER 4

Self-Sufficiency: The Garden

left to right
Michael and David playing on the farm where we lived.

We lived on a small farm with sixty acres and had land available to use. The old farmhouse was complete with mice. There were two bedrooms upstairs (only one was heated), and a kitchen, dining room, living room, and bath downstairs. The house was not insulated, so in the winter when the wind blew, it was really drafty.

There were large black walnut trees in the yard along with a weeping willow and an outhouse for use in the summer and a black hand pump for water in emergencies. There was also a small barn and several rundown sheds. I was happy I had a place to stay with the boys.

Boy, did I need to become self-sufficient. Again, I only had $400 coming in and no job. Everything went to provide a home for my boys and me. I was not about to starve or let my boys go hungry, so I jumped right into being self-sufficient. But that was not as easy as it sounds.

I was raised in a large city, so I knew nothing about gardening, canning, or raising animals, but God gave me the strength and fortitude to learn. My learning curve was very steep. Believe me, I was always praying that we would make it, just the three of us. My parents would have helped if I had asked, but that meant I would have had to move back to Milwaukee. Needless to say, I am a very stubborn person.

The first thing I did was start a garden and learn to can. I had saved enough money to buy seeds, canning jars, and a canner. I had a shovel and a hoe and began to dig a garden in the field next to the house. I would dig small sections at a time in between tending to the boys. They needed a lot of attention since they were both in diapers and loved to run toward the road.

I finally had a large section, fifty foot by fifty foot, and planted everything I could think of: tomatoes, zucchini, beans, carrots, peas, and cucumbers. I dragged hay from the barn and mulched all my plants to keep the weeds down. I was so hungry; I couldn't wait for things to grow. A mother groundhog and her babies were also eyeing my coming produce.

I bought a Ball canning book and began to learn how to can everything I had planted. With what little money I had, I had to make all my own baby food. Actually, it was better for the boys, who never had eaten store-bought baby food.

One of my neighbors, Roger, had extra raspberry plants and gave some of them to me. He farmed only with horses for power. He was a wonderful man who built a beautiful toy barn with working doors for the boys for Christmas. He adorned the barn he made with many hand drawn and painted farm animals. Now our grandchildren play with the barn.

I dug a large plot in back of the house, planted the raspberries, mulched them with hay, and hoped they would grow. They did wonderfully, and we had raspberries the first year. The boys ate all of them right off the plants.

David in the raspberry patch.

Now their children, our grandchildren, do the same thing in our raspberry patch. The joy in watching them run straight for the raspberries and eating them brings back memories of many happy times. Since my raspberry patch has gotten rather large, my boys have used some of my plants to start their own patches at their houses. It is amazing what a child remembers. It was a great tradition to pass on.

(left to right)
David's family in the raspberry patch in 2015.
Jamie, David, and grandsons, Ian and Kyle.

(left to right)
Michael's family in the raspberry patch 2015.
Michael, granddaughter Kaia, Jessica, and granddaughter Karis.

One of my other neighbors tilled up the large field behind the house and planted sweet corn for the neighborhood. I would pick wheelbarrows full of corn and canned all of it. Boy, did it taste good in the winter. I found wild plums along the roadside, and the boys and I picked pails full and took them home. That was the first jelly I made. It looked wonderful, a clear, beautiful ruby red. It also tasted good on warm, homemade bread that I learned to make. Nothing tastes better than bread fresh out of the oven with butter and jelly.

My uncle owned a bakery in my hometown of Milwaukee. I remember walking through it when we visited and seeing all the beautiful desserts. The brownies were my favorite, and still are. He also made the most scrumptious tortes, ones with little meringue mushrooms on top. After he and my aunt sold the bakery and he passed away, my aunt gave me one of his stainless steel mixing bowls. It is still my favorite to this day.

One June day, the boys and I went and picked strawberries at a U-pick farm in the area. That was a fun day. I had decided to make strawberry jam, and the boys were there to help me. Their job was to mash the berries, but they mostly ate them. On my last batch of jam, I turned my back on my oldest son, who was helping me. When I looked back at him, it was hard to hold back the laughter. He was standing on the kitchen table with the bowl of crushed strawberries upside down and on his head! The juice and berries were running down his face and his whole body. What a sight. One I will never forget.

The first year I also started to raise chickens for eggs. My former mother-in-law gave me a few Bantam chickens, as she had extra. I was so excited. I converted the milk house into a chicken coop and put in a ramp for the chickens and a roost. I also put in a fenced enclosure so they would be safe at night from predators. This seemed to work well. The chickens laid eggs, and the boys' job was to gather them.

I remember one of the most perfect days. I was sitting on the front porch, the boys and I were shelling peas, the chickens were running around in the yard, and the sun was shining. All was well with my world.

Michael helping pick beans in the garden.

David picking vegetables for me in the garden.

The garden started yielding produce, and I canned everything I could. Jar after jar of food went on my shelves, as I did not have a separate freezer. I started to feel less stressed; we had a small stockpile of food ready for the winter. We were eating fresh food from the garden that tasted wonderful and was much better than store bought. Why, it tasted so much better because, with all that sweat and hard work, I had grown it!

The boy's father brought over half a deer. I cut up the meat, even though I had no clue how to do so. Again, a very steep learning curve. I was glad when it was all wrapped and in our small refrigerator's freezer. Now we had venison and vegetables to eat.

When fall came, my former mother-in-law gave me some pears and someone else gave me apples and grapes. I canned the pear sauce and applesauce for junior food. I also made grape juice and grape jelly for us to eat.

I was so blessed.

CHAPTER 5

Self-Sufficiency: The Animals

The next year, in spring, I decided to raise pigs. They were the easiest because they grew to maturity before the first hard frost. I bought two piglets (they were the runts of the litter) for five dollars each. On advice from the next-door neighbor, I built a small fenced enclosure on some level ground behind the house and put a large barrel full of hay as a house for the piglets.

It was dusk when I finished and put the piglets into their new enclosure. I was getting the boys ready to go inside for a bath; they were four and five at the time. Out of the corner of my eye, I saw one small piglet run by. *Wait; didn't I just put them in the pen?* Both of those cute little piglets had squeezed through the fence and were running around the yard, followed by my boys.

It was getting dark, and all of us were trying to catch these little piglets. Boy, could they run fast! The boys were laughing and yelling, the piglets were squealing, and I was shouting. What a sight! We finally caught the piglets and put them in the corn crib for the night. The next day, I put chicken wire over the original enclosure. *Let's see if they can get out of this!* I thought. They could not. Trial and error—which was, by all stretch of the imagination, error.

David having fun with the baby pigs.

Michael finding out that piglets can tickle you.

As the pigs grew, I needed to build a larger pen and pig house. I have no idea where I got the strength to haul 4'x 8'x 3/4" used plywood sheets to the new location on a flat area behind the house. I had to go from behind the barn, across the yard, and up a hill to where the new pig house and enclosure would be. My boys were always there to help, but being only four and five, they weren't that strong.

It turned out to be the sturdiest pig house around. The first year we had two pigs, and the last year we had five pigs. I sold four pigs and had enough money to cover the cost of raising five and then had the fifth pig butchered.

CHAPTER 6

Self-Sufficiency: The Honeybees

After learning to raise pigs, I decided to try raising honey bees. Whatever possessed me to try this, I don't know.

I didn't know the first thing about honeybees, so I did a lot of reading on the care of bees. I started with one hive, then two, and finally three. I used package bees to stock the hives. I learned as I went along. I must have had the nicest honeybees; very rarely did I get stung.

I used to love watching them work; in and out of the hive they went from sunup till dusk. I had put the hives behind the barn in a sheltered field, and the hill behind them kept the cold winter winds at bay. They were surrounded by trees, nice and cozy.

Then I decided to add a fourth hive. I actually had found a swarm of bees in the field across the way. *Hey,* I thought, *free bees!* The kids and I grabbed a super, or a bee house, and headed out to the field where the bees were. Supers are wooden boxes that hold a series of framed wax sheets that the bees then make into honeycomb and fill with honey.

The boys sat at a distance while I crawled to the swarm. I figured if I could find the queen and coax her into the super, the rest would follow.

The neighbors must have thought I was an idiot. I had no idea what I was doing, but would you believe, it worked. All the bees entered the super, and I proudly carried them home.

Now that I had all these bees, I needed to purchase a separator to get the honey out of the honeycomb. You only take so much honey from the hives, as the bees need a lot to eat over the winter.

The separator is just a small centrifuge that spins out the honey. You cut off the tops of the honeycombs and then place the framed sheets of comb into the separator. The first time I used the separator, honey spun out and was it beautiful. I had jars and jars of beautiful honey. What I hadn't planned on, though, was the fine mist of honey that covered the walls, cabinets, furniture, and floor of my kitchen. Since the boys were in the kitchen, they were also sticky. It took me days to clean everything.

Self-sufficiency was a lot of trial and error. For me, mostly error—until I got it right.

CHAPTER 7

Self-Sufficiency:
The Great Pumpkin

One year I decided to grow pumpkins for the boys. I was so used to growing only what we needed to eat. We planted the seeds on the edge of the garden next to the raspberries and waited all summer as the pumpkins grew and grew and grew. The boys would check on them daily to make sure they were all right.

By fall we had the most gigantic pumpkin I ever saw. How do we get it from the garden to the fall display of cornstalks? I wondered. We figured since the pumpkins were on top of the hill, we could roll it down. The boys tugged and pulled just to get it out in the open, hard work for two little boys. Still, it hardly moved and was way too big to carry. When they finally got it clear, they just lay on it. They were so tired.

(left to right)
Michael and David trying to roll the great pumpkin out of the weeds.

(left to right)
Michael and David resting after we got the great
pumpkin in the blue plastic snow sled.

We decided to carry the blue plastic snow sled up the hill and forced the pumpkin into it. That took awhile to do. We all were exhausted, but we still had to push and pull the sled with the gigantic pumpkin down the hill.

I wished I had a team of horses. We all pulled and pulled. A couple of hours later, we made it the twenty feet down the hill.

The next year, I grew much smaller pumpkins.

CHAPTER 8

Self-Sufficiency: Other Fun Stuff

There were a lot of long days of work, baking bread to sell, tending to the garden and animals, canning, and gathering eggs. I also made the boys their clothes and toys. I used my old material and made the cutest one-piece outfits. I used whatever I could find to sew into the boys' clothes.

I refinished old furniture that I found at resale shops. I still have some of the pieces, but now they are considered antiques.

We were always active in church. The boys were constantly with me in whatever I did. Their grandparents worked and didn't have time to babysit. I made sure the boys received a good Christian foundation so in bad times they could count on their faith. I sang in the choir, and all the children of the choir members sat in the front pew. They were always (mostly) on their best behavior. Everyone at church was always very supportive and kind. We had a lot of fun and made many friends.

You treasure each moment. Even the smallest accomplishments are great in your eyes, like the boys' first fish that they caught, the dogs, Tuffy and Rowdy, that spent a lot of time keeping the boys safe and out of trouble, and the boys' homemade fort with the prized beaver log.

(left to right)
Michael and David with David's prized first fish that he caught.

(left to right)
Michael and David with Rowdy and Tuffy, the
faithful dogs that kept watch over the boys.

David and Michael in their newly constructed
fort with their prized beaver log.

It was a wonderful and peaceful lifestyle. Being self-sufficient really makes you appreciate what you have. There is a lot of hard work involved, but the joy is in the accomplishment of the impossible.

Never in my wildest dreams did I ever picture myself gardening, canning, and raising animals for food. The hardest part was learning to butcher chickens. Someone had to show me how to kill and clean them, and I learned to chop off the heads. I put my old copper boiler over a fire to heat water for dipping and defeathering. Then I had to clean the insides, singe the stray feathers with a match, cool them down, wrap, and freeze them. I learned never to name any farm animals because then I would cry while killing them. I had to remember I was putting food on our table.

I constantly remembered my father and grandmother and all that they went through, so I figured I could do the same. It didn't hurt me; I gained a tremendous amount of knowledge.

God seems to have blessed me with a spirit that never gives up. What I tried did not always work, but I always kept trying. God blessed my garden, and it produced more food than we could eat, preserve, or give away.

CHAPTER 9

The Prairie

I eventually took a course on native prairies and got hooked. It was my entertainment since my budget was very limited. The instructor was kind enough to show me where all the prairies and different prairie plants were in my area. I started going out with my boys and taking pictures. That developed into educational slide shows and art shows. It was also good exercise. I had no formal training in photography, but I was always looking for that amazing picture.

I took many pictures of my boys looking at the prairie plants, hoping someday to write a book. I started a prairie nursery and sold seeds and plants. It was another way to make some money. Twenty years later, I eventually wrote a children's educational book on native prairies of Wisconsin called *A Child's View of a Prairie*. It is a children's field guide to Wisconsin prairies. I used some of the pictures I had taken, including some of the boys. God sure has made a beautiful world.

By this time, we had moved from the country to a house in Waterloo, Wisconsin, a small farm town. I had extra land next to the house and planted a large garden and a large plot for my prairie seeds. I also started back to work at a country store in town that was right up my alley. It sold everything you would need to be self-sufficient. I was in heaven. They even sold my seeds.

I could tell you that I sat around reading my Bible all day, but I didn't. I didn't read it at all. Still, God found time to take care of the boys and me. I had to make an effort to not feel sorry for myself. What I learned from this experience was not to give up, even though I wanted to many times, especially when I was tired and lonely. We had a roof over our heads, more food than we needed, and, best of all, we had each other. Life was good.

CHAPTER 10

The Big Mistake

Sometimes life takes a turn in a totally opposite direction from what you had planned or dreamed. You think you are making wise decisions, and God is looking down on your foolishness.

It is not human nature to admit we are truly stupid. I think when everything is going wrong is when we really grow the most. I know I did. All those years working on the small farm helped the healing process. I didn't have time to think, for I was way too tired. Yet the years went by, and the heartache of divorce was healed.

It was still very hard being a single mother. I started back to work, earning enough to pay for childcare. I never earned enough, though, and the small amount of child support didn't make any difference. But I kept trying, moving forward and getting better jobs.

I was very shy and didn't date much at all. I was more comfortable in my own little world, working. Needless to say, I was still extremely naive.

My sister, who is the opposite of me, decided to set me up on a blind date with one of her friends. That should have raised many red flags, but I trusted her. The man turned out to be charming and wonderful—almost too good to be true. After not dating for about ten years, having someone interested in me felt amazing. We dated for a while, and he seemed perfect.

Then he asked me to marry him.

He also wanted to buy a small farm in a neighboring town, but his money was tied up in property that hadn't yet sold. I had some savings, so we were married and used my money to buy the farm. But after only three months into the marriage, I found out that he was a con artist and that my sister had told him I had some savings. He had no land or money and was now working on the next woman to con.

I had to use the rest of my savings to undo this mess. I lost the farm, and the boys and I moved into an apartment. Could my life get any harder or depressing? God seemed to be stripping me of everything. I was not mad at God, though; I was angry with myself for trusting my sister.

That part of my life I would like to forget, but God uses my mistakes for His reasons, even though I am still wondering why.

PART 2

Dreams from God

CHAPTER 11

The Unexpected Dream

The boys were in high school when something unexpected and amazing happened. And I really mean unexpected.

The boys had gone hunting with their father and I was home alone in November 1990. One night, I had a dream, but it was not your normal dream. It had two parts, each of them a snapshot. In the first part of the dream, I was standing in and looking out at a long rectangular banquet hall. On my right was an enclosed serving buffet with a kitchen to the right of that. In the banquet hall were a lot of tables arranged in a slanted position with men, women, and children standing around. In the middle of the room was a man with people standing around him. There was no movement. Just this peaceful snapshot.

The banquet hall and the man in the middle.

In the second part of the dream, I was in an off-white room, not the banquet hall. I did not see any windows, yet the room was lighted. I was standing in front of the same man from the first part of the dream, looking at his left hand. He was standing next to a square column, which was on his right, and on the little finger of his left hand was a ring surrounded by red. I stared at the ring for what seemed like a long time. I then looked at his face but did not see it. I looked into his eyes but did not see them; instead, I was overcome with the love, joy, and peace pouring into me from his eyes. It was like I was seeing God.

This is the hardest thing to explain. There are not enough adjectives to describe it. I was seeing but not seeing, only overwhelmed by love, kindness, peace, and indescribable joy. For what seemed like a lifetime, God's attributes poured into me. There was such depth and fullness and a glory beyond my comprehension—a glorious, harmonious whole. It was so intense I could not stand it. Yet I wanted it to go on, but I also wanted it to end. Then it finally did end.

The square column, the man, and the special ring.

Wow! How do you process this type of event? I had no idea what I had just experienced. Why had God let me experience this? I was trying to think where this took place and who this man was. What was I supposed to do with this? I knew this was not an ordinary dream, but what was it? It was etched on my mind.

I went to church thinking that maybe this man was at church, but no one there was even similar. And where was this banquet hall? Nothing in my town or where I worked was similar. I did not tell anyone about this. Who would have believed me? It definitely did not come with any instructions. God could have given me an instruction manual or maybe just a little hint!

I've often wondered if I'm the only person something like this has happened to. Twenty years later, upon writing this account, I did some research and found that something similar had happened to Charles Grandison Finney, leader of the Second Great Awakening and president of Oberlin College in Oberlin, Ohio. Following is his account from *Memoirs of Rev. Charles G. Finney (1876)*:

> I received a mighty baptism of the Holy Ghost. Without any expectation of it, without ever having the thought in my mind that there was any such thing for me, without any recollection that I had ever heard the thing mentioned by any person in the world, the Holy Spirit descended upon me in a manner that seemed to go through me, body and soul. I could feel the impression, like a wave of electricity going through and through me. Indeed it seemed to come in waves and waves of liquid love; for I could not express it in any other way.

It seemed like the very breath of God. I can recollect distinctly that it seemed to fan me, like immense wings.

No words can express the wonderful love that was shed abroad in my heart. I wept aloud with joy and love; and I do not know but I should say, I literally bellowed out the unutterable gushing of my heart. These waves came over me, and over me, and over me, one after the other, until I recollect I cried out, "I shall die if these waves continue to pass over me." I said, "Lord, I cannot bear any more;" yet I had no fear of death …

This was the same overwhelming, intense emotion I felt, but mine came through a person I had not yet met.

As time went on, I stopped looking for the man and the place. The dream was still fresh in my mind, but I was not going crazy looking for him.

CHAPTER 12

The Promise

I had the boys to raise, my work, and all the daily chores. By this time, the child support had been drastically reduced for each child, my job at the bank did not pay very much, and our budget was very tight.

I was going in the hole financially and could not make ends meet. I had used all my savings to pay the bills I was left with from the farm. What was I to do? My whole family had moved fifteen hundred miles away to Clearwater, Florida, and I was left with no moral support.

I prayed about what to do. I either had to go more in debt to survive or move in with my parents who lived far away so I could earn enough to support my boys. This was the worst time of my life. I kept praying and received no answer. I was pretty self-sufficient and did not want to ask for help. Nor did I believe in food stamps or welfare.

What to do? I remembered the story of the fleece in Judges 6:36–40, where Gideon wanted to make sure this message was from God:

> Gideon said to God, "If you will save Israel by my hand
> as you have promised—look, I will place a wool fleece
> on the threshing floor. If there is dew only on the fleece

and all the ground is dry, then I will know that you will save Israel by my hand, as you said." And that is what happened. Gideon rose early the next day; he squeezed the fleece and wrung out the dew—a bowlful of water. Then Gideon said to God, "Do not be angry with me. Let me make just one more request. Allow me one more test with the fleece. This time make the fleece dry and the ground covered with dew." That night God did so. Only the fleece was dry; all the ground was covered with dew.

I decided that if it worked for Gideon, maybe it would work for me. It was a poor analogy for me, but it was the only thing in the Bible I could remember that kind of fit my situation.

I felt like I was trying to bargain with God. Finally, I told God that if the child support was stopped, I would leave the boys with their father, move over fifteen hundred miles away, live with my parents, work three jobs to raise enough money to support my sons, and then come back.

I was thinking that only God can stop a garnishment.

And guess what? The garnishment stopped! I could not get it started by calling or writing every government agency or organization I could find. I think I cried more while making the decision to move than in all the rest of my life. I promised God that I would go, so how could I break that promise? This was one of the hardest tests of my faith.

It was horrible leaving my boys with their father. He was a nice guy, but I knew he would not take care of them like I would. But my parents would not let them come with me.

I talked with my minister; he was kind, of course, but was absolutely no help. My boys were equally in turmoil. The security they had had their whole life was leaving. We all cried. I was scared because everything was out of my control. I so wanted to go back on my promise. But I kept remembering, "Have faith and trust in the Lord."

I then quit my job, left my boys and my friends, and moved to Florida. Once there, I got three jobs and worked myself sick. It was the only way I could cope with the separation.

I prayed that God would take care of my boys while I was away. Of course, I had people tell me that I was a bad parent—something I did not need to hear. I already felt like a failure.

CHAPTER 13

Dream Becomes Reality

I started going to a conservative Lutheran church in Clearwater, but not my parents' Lutheran church. I enjoyed the new church, sang in the choir, and went to Bible studies. I was starting to cope with being away from my boys. By this time, the dream I had in November 1990 was way back in my memory.

Why I did not go to my parents' church, I have no idea. But one day, I decided to and went by myself. My parents were out of town. I entered the church and sat down. The church was a long rectangular building filled with pews.

When the minister got up to preach, I noticed that he had a small ring on the little finger of his left hand. The minute I looked at him, the dream came rushing back. This was the man in the dream! I sat through the church service, stunned. When the service ended, I left. I did not even shake the minister's hand on the way out.

I thought, *What am I supposed to do now? A minister, of all people!* Why the heck did it have to be a minister? Could not God have given me a dream about an ordinary guy? I went to church my whole life, always thinking that ministers are holy and close to God. I wasn't even close to being holy, nor was I close to God. And I sure wasn't versed in the Bible even though I attended church regularly. Still, I kept going to that church for a while and did my best to avoid the minister. Where is that instruction book when I need it?

I was still working three jobs and had saved enough money to go back home. That was my dream, but not God's. Going home was all I thought about. But the boys needed cars to get to work so they could earn enough money for food, so I used all my money to buy them vehicles.

I missed them terribly, but now I did not have enough money to go home. So I moved into a condo and continued working to save up again. I was lonely, tired, depressed, and confused.

After several weeks of going to my parents' church, I decided to tell them about the dream I had had several years earlier. They thought I was nuts. My own parents did not believe me! My whole life I had tried to be good and not lie, so why would I lie about something this amazing?

I had trouble understanding what was happening to me. What to do? I knew the dream was real; I could still see and feel it clearly. Why didn't my parents believe me?

CHAPTER 14

Meeting Takes Place

Soon after telling my parents, I was awakened one night by someone calling my name. I then knew it was all right to tell the minister about my dream.

Remember, I did not read my Bible. Sure, I went to church, but that was it. So how could I tell a minister about my dream? Some ministers think this stuff does not occur in this day and age. They are happy keeping God in a box. Plus my parents told me not to tell the minister, for he would think I was nuts.

But the feeling got stronger and stronger in the coming weeks, so I decided, against everyone's better judgment, to make an appointment with the minister. He was known *not* to keep appointments, so I figured that if he kept the appointment, I would tell him about the dream.

He kept the appointment.

The day of the appointment arrived, March 25, 1992. I was so nervous I almost did not go. But the prompting was so strong that, against my better judgment, I went to the appointment. The first thing he said was "You can't tell me anything I haven't heard before." I was thinking, *Want to bet?*

I started telling him about the dream I had had almost eighteen months earlier. The first part of the dream I was standing and looking out at a long rectangular banquet hall. On my right was an enclosed serving buffet with a kitchen to the right of that. In the banquet hall were a lot of tables arranged in a slanted position with men, women, and children standing around. In the middle of the room was a man with people standing around him.

In the second part of the dream I was in an off white room, not the banquet hall. I did not see any windows yet the room was lighted. I was standing in front of the same man looking at his left hand. He was standing next to a square column, which was on his right, and on the little finger of his left hand was a ring surrounded with red. I stared at the ring for what seemed like a long time. I remember looking up at his face but not seeing it. I looked into his eyes, but not seeing his eyes, instead I was overcome with the glory of love, joy and peace pouring into me from his eyes. It was like seeing God. It is the hardest thing to explain. There are not enough adjectives to describe it. I was seeing but not seeing, only feeling overwhelming love, kindness, peace, indescribable joy. For what seemed like a lifetime God's attributes poured into me. There was such depth, fullness and a glory beyond my comprehension – a glorious harmonious whole. It was so intense that I could not stand it, I wanted it to go on but I also wanted it to end.

I figured the dream was telling me that the man was a minister, a man of God. That was the only thing that made any sense to me.

After I finished, the minister just stared at me. He then asked, "Which ring was it?" He had a ring on each hand. I said, "The one on your little finger." He then became emotional. No, *emotional* is not the right word. He was stunned.

Then he asked, "Are you an angel?" I said, "I am *not* an angel." (Besides, I had a cold, and angels don't get sick!) "I am just telling you an unusual dream." I could not even quote a Bible verse let alone make sense of any of this. Then he told me that he was not supposed to get the ring and that it was from an uncle who had premonitions.

Only God could have known about his uncle's premonitions. I had neither met the minister nor any of his family. The minister was not supposed to get the ring, but God saw to it that he did. The ring was so prominent in the dream.

Looking back, I realize that God showed me things that were to come. It is amazing how God orchestrates all of this. The timing is always perfect. I am finding out that there are no coincidences when God is in control.

But where was I when I saw the minister and looked into his eyes? I was in an off-white room. I did not see any windows, and we were standing next to a square column. Why a square column? The column was as prominent as the ring. This was a place I did not recognize.

After my talk with the minister, I left, thinking that that was all I had to do. But my dream had not completely happened yet. Was I doing this all wrong?

I had so many questions, but who to ask? I could not ask another minister; they all seemed to put parameters on God. They were also very skeptical, and with good reason. This only happens in the Bible, not in this day and age. I remember thinking, *Why me? I am not even versed in the Bible. Why did I have to leave my kids, my job, and my home just to deliver this message? Could God not have found someone else?*

CHAPTER 15

Constant Prayer

I found out that the minister was divorced. What was even more unusual was that he was from my home state. What were the odds? There were a lot of rumors going around about him, which I did not want hear. What I saw in him was the most beautiful spirit, beyond anything that the world would ever know. That's what I always had to keep in my mind.

On April 6, 1992, I felt the need to pray for him. It was such a strong urge; I felt connected to him. It was like plugging in a lamp and turning it on—as long as it was plugged in, the light shined. Well, I was plugged into his spirit and did not have a way to unplug. You cannot pull out a plug you cannot see. I did not ask for this to happen, and I can't explain it.

Who was I to pray for him? I thought I only had to tell him the dream and then I would be off the hook. I had not received the all-important instruction manual. I prayed most evenings and I prayed a lot when I had to leave my children. Other than that, I did not pray continuously. I didn't even know the minister personally. But all my spare time I seemed to want to pray, which was very unusual for me. I didn't even know what I was to pray about. So I decided to pray for his healing. I knew he was divorced; maybe he was having trouble coming to terms with it.

On April 19, Easter Sunday, the urge left me, like becoming unplugged. I was finally peaceful. Thank heavens, because I was getting exhausted and sick.

Everything went well for a couple of weeks. What a great joy that was!

CHAPTER 16

God's Voice

I was back to normal, working, working, and working. It was better than eating and crying. I had made some friends to go out with and finally had some semblance of a life.

One of my friends confided in me that she had a crush on the minister and was bound and determined to go out with him. Since she was a friend, I wished her well in her efforts. I only had a spiritual connection with him. I thought to help him heal. I was not dating him. I didn't want to interfere in his life anymore than I had to. Not having an instruction manual was really hard. Only God had a clue as to what was going on. I just wanted to go back home.

I was at my second job, J. Byrons, a department store, arguing with myself. I had no idea what I was doing or if I needed to do something else for the minister. He made me so nervous every time I spoke with him. I felt like such an idiot when I told him the dream. Sometimes I have a tendency to overthink a situation.

This was all so new, and I had no one to confide in. I was sitting in the back office alone. There were no customers in sight, when this loud voice from nowhere said, "Have patience, My child." Instantly, this beautiful peace washed over me from head to toe, and I started to cry. Every bit of stress left my body. It was indescribably beautiful. I was wondering if anyone else had heard the voice, as it was rather loud but gentle, fatherly.

Where did that voice come from? No one was anywhere near the customer service area. Was God speaking to me? The minute I heard the voice, the peace I felt let me know that I didn't have to worry or try so hard anymore. Why did He choose to speak to me? I don't know.

Ever since that day, I have had enormous patience—almost. Patience is really hard for me; I like things to get done quickly. Even though the peace I felt was unbelievable, it did not last as long as I wanted, with daily life interfering all the time.

I still was not reading my Bible, even though I now felt as if I were walking through the Old Testament. People having prophetic dreams and hearing voices were not very prevalent that I knew of.

And the minister was of no help. What would he think if I told him I now heard the voice of God? I don't drink, and the only pills I took were multivitamins. I was wondering how much weirder things could get. I really needed a friend who had a relationship with God to talk to. The minister was very private and emotionally closed. Plus, I was a member of his congregation. As much as I needed a friend to talk to, he was out of bounds. My parents were of even less help.

Who did I have to turn to? The voice I heard could have said something else besides "Have patience, My child," like "You are on the right track" or "The instruction manual is in the mail."

"Have patience, My child" seemed to cover a lot of territory.

CHAPTER 17

Unexpected Second Dream

Everything settled down till the middle of May. I was working, going out with some girlfriends, and singing in choir. It was finally peaceful, and I was not fretting about the minister. Plus, he seemed to be the exact opposite of me. He had his life, and I had mine. I was finally done.

Little did I know that this would never be finished until the second half of the first dream occurred. Someday I would see God's overwhelming beautiful spirit in the minister.

Then on May 6, 1992, while peacefully sleeping, I had another two-part dream. In the first part, I was standing next to Jesus. I didn't want to look, but I felt so very safe. How I knew who was standing next to me, I don't know. I just knew. I was looking out into a dark room when all of a sudden many faces came out of the darkness. They were women's faces that were ugly and distorted. I had no idea who they were. I did not recognize any of them. In the darkness behind the faces was a spirit in turmoil. It was wrestling with something, some problem. I thought it was the minister. No other person came to mind. But I was safe and calm next to Jesus.

Looking into the darkness with distorted
women's faces coming toward me.

In the second part of the dream, I was floating outside of our church looking down through a window at a man kneeling at the communion railing, praying. There were cushions around the communion railing, and the man was kneeling on the second or third cushion from the left side of the altar. In front of the kneeling figure was a tall, thin figure in glowing white. I remember thinking that the glowing figure was standing right where the baptismal font was in church, even though I could not see it.

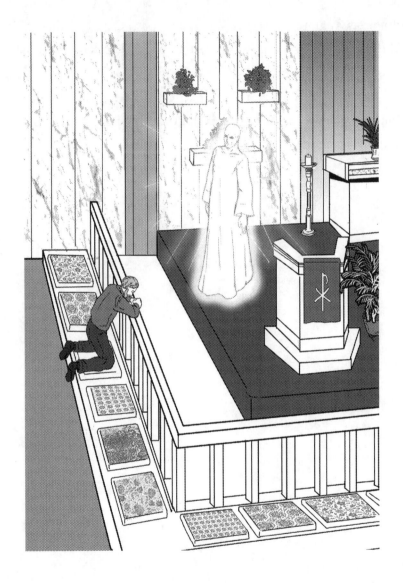

Looking down into the church at the minister kneeling
with a tall, glowing figure in front of him.

Was this the Holy Spirit? I was thinking, *Baptism and the Holy Spirit go together.* But I should not have been able to see the Holy Spirit unless I was dead. I knew it was a spiritual being standing over the minister. It could have been an angel sent by God.

I floating outside of the church. The whole scene was calm, peaceful, and surreal. Then I woke up.

Now what was I supposed to do with this dream? Why did I have it? I assumed it had something to do with the minister. Since I was watching these two separate scenes play out and was entirely calm and peaceful, I knew it didn't have anything to do with me.

I didn't want to make an appointment with the minister. What a coward I was. Plus, I thought an appointment would take too long. I had this sense of urgency because of the first part of the dream. If the minister was in turmoil or wrestling with something, I did not want to take my sweet time in getting him to church where I knew he would be safe.

I had the music director at the church call and tell him to go to church and pray. I figured that the dream was telling me that the minister was in turmoil and needed to be at church. The director called me back after talking to the minister, who said he was sick and wasn't going to church. I was panicking by now; there was such a sense of urgency about the dream. I called the music director again and told her to tell him he better get to church right away. When she called me back, she said he was going to church.

I still cannot believe he went. Why didn't I call him directly? Maybe I did not want to talk to him and try to explain my dream until after he went to church. I had thought I was done with whatever was going on. I was still a coward, but I was in good company. Many people in the Bible also hesitated. Take Jonah. At least I wasn't swallowed by a large fish.

The minister spent the day in the sanctuary praying. The music director said he had received some Scripture from the book of Haggai and saw a perfect circle with the colors of the rainbow inside.

I thought I had better read the book of Haggai. I had to figure out where it was in the New or Old Testament since I still had not cracked open my Bible. God had picked the most unspiritual person he could find, and probably also the dumbest.

This is what my feeble mind figured out after researching. The key concepts in the book of Haggai are that spiritual restoration must precede social or political restoration and that God's presence is the key to restoration. Following are some important key teachings about God:

- God expects to be our highest priority always.
- God remains with His people even when they are under discipline or judgment.

Okay, so what did this have to do with the minister? I had no clue.

I read the short book of Haggai, and several passages jumped out at me. I am sure the minister got something entirely different from it. Haggai 1:5–7 says,

Now this is what the Lord Almighty says: "Give careful thought to your ways. You have planted much, but have harvested little. You eat, but never have enough. You drink, but never have your fill. You put on clothes, but are not warm. You earn wages, only to put them in a purse with holes in it." This is what the Lord Almighty says: "Give careful thought to your ways."

Maybe the minister was not living up to God's expectations of him, although his sermons were very good. In my first dream, I saw the attributes of God in him. It was beyond belief. But I never saw it when I met with him.

The second passage, Haggai 2:20–23, seemed to jump out at me:

The word of the Lord came to Haggai a second time on the twenty-fourth day of the month: "Tell Zerubbabel governor of Judea that I will shake the heavens and the earth. I will overturn royal thrones and shatter the power of the foreign. I will overthrow chariots and their drivers; horses and their riders will fall, each by the sword of his brother. On that day," declares the Lord Almighty, "I will take you, my servant Zerubbabel son of Shealtiel," declares the Lord, "and I will make you like my signet ring, for I have chosen you," declares the Lord Almighty.

Maybe God someday will shake the heavens and the earth and will choose this minister for a special task. What task I don't know.

CHAPTER 18

The Talk

How often does God take such special notice of two people? He did in the Old and New Testaments, but in this day and age? What was coming in the future that required so much preparation?

Should I have mulled over this dream for weeks before telling the minister to go to church right away? Where was my patience? I figured that if God chose me, He knew I would react to the dream and not wait. Since God is all-knowing, I went with my first reaction, and that was to keep the minister safe.

God has always been ten steps ahead of me. If the minister did not listen and go to church, he would not have received this Scripture. The first dream must have had an impact on him, for he did listen to my request.

This whole spiritual adventure was frustrating. I needed to talk it over with someone, so I called for an appointment with the minister at my previous church. When the day came, I could not help but be apprehensive. I figured he was going to think I was a little touched, but I still needed to talk to someone. It was not easy doing something like this alone. I knew that God was with me and the Holy Spirit was guiding me, but I needed some human encouragement.

The minister and I had a good discussion. He did not laugh at me or put me down. Not that he understood what was happening to me, but he was receptive to the dreams I had had and the voices I had heard.

He did relate a story to me about a spiritual encounter he once had. While driving in a car, he heard the words, "Only you can give your heart to God. You cannot give someone else's heart." He said he was scared to look next to him, where the voice had come. He was worried about a special person who he believed was not saved.

It was helpful to speak to someone of authority who had also heard a voice. Now I did not feel so alone. I learned that I could only share what I saw with the minister and pray. He always had the choice whether to believe me or not.

God had said, "Have patience, My child." This covered a whole host of situations and problems. Patience for the minister, my children, my parents, my work, or myself? Which one was it? Or was it all of them? Finally, God told me to have patience for the minister. The minister must have needed more spiritual growth before I would be able to see what I saw in the dream.

I knew that God doesn't make mistakes. He is very orderly and knows already what is going to happen. I always had a choice whether to tell the minister or not, and he had a choice whether to believe or not. Doesn't it seem so simple?

CHAPTER 19

My Hope

During the next month, I went to church and didn't have any discussions with the minister. I still felt unqualified for this mission, or whatever you would call it. I would listen to the sermons on Sunday. They were interesting, but I just was not excited about them. And I still didn't have time to read my Bible. You'd think I would have been so interested in reading the whole Bible, but I just did not have time. I was usually so tired after working thirteen hours a day and doing my home chores that I didn't want to do anything. I guess I didn't want to think about what it said.

Back to reality and my life. The church was expanding and in the process of building a new church. The church council had discussions on what to do with the existing church building, whether to make it into a fellowship hall, offices, or Sunday school rooms. The fellowship hall won. So all of the pews were removed, painting was completed, new carpeting was put down, and a new kitchen with a rolling serving counter was designed and built. When the tables were set in the room, this looked so familiar to me. But something was not right. Wait, stop! It was my dream, but the tables were not placed correctly. They were in straight rows, not diagonally. Plus, in my dream there were a lot of men, women, and children at some kind of gathering.

Wow, my dream did have a chance of happening, and now I knew where! I knew if the dream or premonition was from God, it would happen. Now I needed to know when.

"Have patience, My child" came to mind. This would have been easier if I had had a manual and a definite timetable. But no such luck. I was winging it, no matter how bad a job I did or how much I messed up. I had to remember that it was God's plan, not mine.

Why did God pick me? Did He know from the beginning of my life that this adventure would come to pass at this particular time? Just thinking about this and how all the people I meet are interwoven by God's hand is mind-boggling.

Meanwhile, the minister to whom I had given the message was very antagonistic. His sermons were good on the Holy Spirit and communication and trust in God, but I was not seeing what I had seen in my first dream.

It was frustrating knowing that what I saw and experienced in the dream about the minister was different from the worldly view. So many times I wanted to step in and shake him. I could see it so clearly. If only he could understand what I saw in him. Where was the joy, the love, and the peace? Where was the beautiful spirit? But I could not make him see what I saw in the dream. It was his decision what to do with the information I provided.

We were way past the "forty days and nights" concept.

The beginning of July, things settled down for me. Work was going well, but I missed being with my children. I still felt guilty about leaving them. I don't think I will ever get over the time I lost with my boys. I can never get that back. I missed my oldest son's graduation from high school and their football games and growing up. I was brought up in a family that kept their emotions secret. Who was I to speak about the sorrow I kept inside?

I was still connected to the minister, but he was not connected to me in the same way. If only he would have sensed how frustrating this was for me and how much I needed a friend. He never spoke about what he was feeling. He never opened up and just talked to me. I was thinking that maybe everything was done, but my first dream had not yet happened.

"Have patience, My child."

CHAPTER 20

The Command

On July 29, 1992, while sleeping, I remember being in a light gray, calming expanse of nothing. I was in a most restful, sheltered place, even though it was an endless space. Then suddenly, a loud and commanding voice broke into my sleep, saying, "Romans six eight."

Instantly awake, I turned on my bedside light and glanced at the clock. It was 3:28 a.m. I opened my Bible to Romans 6:8 and read, "Now if we died with Christ, we believe that we will also live with him."

I was shaken but hyper at the same time. What had happened? I was in the nice, restful place. Was I the only one who heard this booming voice? Why 3:28 in the morning? I had to go to work for thirteen hours that day. What was I supposed to do? What did dying with Christ mean?

I needed to think about it. Was this message for the minister or just for me? Was this what the Holy Spirit sounded like? It was so different from the voice of God that said, "Have patience, My child." That voice was kind and reassuring, and the moment I heard it, an amazing peace washed over me. But this voice was commanding and forceful; the Holy Spirit, I believe. It would have been nice if the voice had said, "This is the Holy Spirit. Please read Romans chapter six verse eight." But then I might have taken my sweet time in doing so.

I pondered on Romans 6:8 for a week to no avail. What was supposed to happen? I did not have a clue. To cover my bases, I called the minister and let him know what had happened. He didn't have a clue either. But he said he was really spiritually restless the night it happened to me. Why was he spiritually restless while I was tired and calm? I definitely was not expecting a loud, booming, and commanding voice that night. I told him maybe he should read Romans 6:8 also. It is amazing how the Holy Spirit can use the most naive and dumb person.

By the end of the week, I felt that I should read Romans chapters six through eight instead of limiting my reading to Romans 6:8 and decided to get the largest commentary on these chapters I could find. I found an expositional commentary called *Romans, Volume 2 The Reign of Grace (Romans 5–8)* by James Montgomery Boice.

I skipped Romans 5 and started reading Romans 6. "Shall we go on sinning so that grace may increase? By no means! We died to sin; how can we live in it any longer?" (v. 1)

Sin and grace. Had I died to sin? We are absolved of our sins every Sunday in church. Was this not enough? I didn't know. I had so many questions. I don't think I ever learned what this meant in church. This was getting so complicated. I was working three jobs and trying to study every spare second.

At the end of studying Romans 6, another interesting and weird encounter happened. On August 8, I awoke, sat up in bed, and knew that someone was in my condo. I wasn't scared, which seemed odd. It was dark, but I could sense someone walking toward my bedroom from the kitchen. But I didn't see anyone.

Suddenly, I felt someone sit down on the bed next to me. There was no one there, yet the mattress sank. I am not kidding; the mattress sank just like someone had sat down. It is hard to describe something I could not see, but I could feel the presence of someone. Then the presence lay down next to me. Whatever it was seemed to be in enormous turmoil. Instinctively, I laid down and put my arm around it for comfort and fell sound asleep.

I woke up in the morning thinking, *That was weird.* Maybe weird does not even cover it. But this was not any stranger than anything else that was happening to me. I was connected to the minister, but this was not him. I was not dealing well with what God had given me so far, and I truly did not need anything else. I didn't know that it would be awhile before this puzzle piece would be revealed.

Meanwhile, I went back to reading Romans. When I got to the chapter titled "Whatever Became of Sin?" in Romans 7 and read about the commandments, something happened.

On Tuesday, August 11, 1992, I had never felt so bad in my life. I had to face all the sin I had ever committed and found out how much it had hurt God. I was curled up in a ball, crying my heart out. Thinking about sin is something I have always avoided. I was trying to excuse it away and definitely did not want to think that God had seen all the bad along with the good. I had always thought I was a good person, going to church and trying to live a good life. But my thinking that I am good means nothing. Really looking at my sinful nature was a rude awakening. Is this what they call dying to Christ?

In his book, Pastor James Montgomery Boice quoted Karl Menninger, founder of the world-renowned Menninger Clinic in Topeka, Kansas. He said Menninger argued sin has been redefined: first, as crime—that is, as transgression of the law of man rather than transgression of the law of God—and second, as symptoms. Since "symptoms" are caused by things external to the individual, they are seen as effects for which the offender is not responsible. Thus it happened that sin against God has been redefined (and dismissed) as the unfortunate effects of bad circumstances. And no one is to blame.

Yet sin is sin—and we are to blame. Sin, whether we acknowledge it or not, really is "any want of conformity unto or transgression of the law of God" (The Westminster Shorter Catechism, Answer 14).

After reading this, I knew in my heart that I had dismissed sin and figured I was not responsible for it. I sure was wrong. I *was* responsible for my actions and my sins against God. That week, every sin I had committed I seemed to remember and asked for forgiveness. It was very exhausting but liberating. I had to face my sinful nature. I was dying to Christ.

I totally forgot about the minister. In reading Romans 6 and 7, I felt this was about me and I did not have to deal with anyone else. Yet I still had to read Romans 8.

Therefore, there is now no condemnation for those who are in Christ Jesus, because through Christ Jesus the law of the Spirit of life set me free from the law of sin and death. For what the law was powerless to do in that it was weakened by the sinful nature, God did by sending his own Son in the likeness of sinful man to be a sin offering. And so he condemned sin in sinful man, in order that the righteous requirements of the law might be fully met in us, who do not live according to the sinful nature but according to the Spirit. (vv. 1–4)

Was I living in the Spirit now? I still did not know what I was searching for. What was I supposed to learn? All I knew was that the voice was loud and commanding: "Romans six eight."

I read and studied further into Romans 8. Then I read Romans 8:28–30:

And we know that in all things God works for the good of those who love him, who have been called according to his purpose. For those God foreknew he also predestined to be conformed to the likeness of his Son, that he might be the firstborn among many brothers. And those he predestined, he also called; those he called, he also justified; those he justified, he also glorified.

What came over me next is hard to describe. It was like being in a fog and then in an instant everything became clear. The words in the Bible came alive. It was the most exciting thing that ever happened to me. The words in the Bible were understandable. Finally, it wasn't just a dull, old book.

The experience was so different from the dreams I had or the voices I heard. I was so excited and could not wait to tell someone. I called my parents and explained everything. They thought I had joined a cult and did not have the faintest idea of what I was talking about. I thought at least they would be happy and excited for me.

I called the minister; he was a little more excited. But I don't think he understood what I was trying to explain. He was going on about how different our personalities were. So many strange and unusual things were happening to me, but I could not grasp them. How could anyone else understand? The Holy Spirit would have to enlighten them. All I know was that I was so excited about the Bible. I could not find anyone who was interested. I thanked God for what He had done. The Holy Spirit had given me the understanding of what it meant to be saved.

CHAPTER 21

Excitement to Read

There was no stopping me after this. I had an insatiable hunger to read.

I went to the library at our church, but found it was almost nonexistent. Where was I supposed to find books to read? A friend at work suggested I come to her church library. When I walked into it, I was overwhelmed. It was like heaven on earth. I had never seen so many books to read.

They graciously let me take out books, but I felt I could only read certain ones. These are some of the books I was led to read: *The Cost of Discipleship* by Dietrich Bonhoeffer, *The Salvation of the Soul* by Watchman Nee, *The Holiness of God* by RC Sproul, and *The Person and Work of the Holy Spirit* by R.A. Torrey.

There were many, many other books by authors like Martin Luther, John MacArthur, Woodrow Kroll, and Charles Spurgeon. And the list goes on and on.

I read continually after work for many months. I did not watch television. Instead, I sat down with popcorn and one of the books. These are some of the topics I studied: intercessory prayer, predestination, the Trinity, the Holy Spirit, angels, the attributes of God, and salvation. I even bought a systematic theology book to study. Why was I studying so much? I had no idea.

I kept going to church and listening to the sermons that were good, but they were not telling me if the minister was finally figuring this out. The sermons were on aging, Jesus, prayer, and worry.

Sometimes I knew when the minister was not doing well. Other times some kind of sign would have been nice, anything would have been encouraging. When there was a sermon on Romans 7 and 8, I thought the minister had finally gotten the message that God had for him. But unfortunately, his eyes were still guarded and dull. I did not see a crack in his worldly exterior that would let out that overwhelmingly beautiful spirit. I was at a loss as to what to do and how long this would take. I was hoping it would not be like in the Bible, where everything seemed to take forty days, forty weeks, or forty years. I dreaded the forty-year scenario, as I was already forty-four years old.

Maybe I wasn't supposed to be there, I thought. Looking back on the second dream, I was outside the church looking in. Perhaps I was away from the church, and this was God's way of telling me that He was taking care of it and I did not have to be there.

I tried to keep tabs on the minister one way or another. I was still at church, singing in the choir and helping with Sunday school, and could sense when the minister was peaceful or not. That was weird. How I knew something was not right I had no idea. But since God and the Holy Spirit seemed to pop in and out of my life, I wasn't going to question it anymore. I really wanted to have my life back, whatever it is. I was so hoping the minister would just figure it out.

"Have patience, My child."

CHAPTER 22

The Fire

With all this going on, I have no idea how I functioned. I was excited and tired but mostly confused. Why was this happening to me? I am just an ordinary person, trying to make it in this world.

Raising kids from a long distance is extremely hard. I was always scared that something would happen to them, especially in the old farmhouse where they were living with their dad. Always on my mind was that the house might burn down. I prayed that God would take care of them since I could not.

Then I received a call from my oldest son telling me that his bedroom had caught fire and that both of their bedrooms had burned up. Little did I know that I was the cause of the fire! I had sent my boys a care package of cookies, and my oldest son put his under the table next to his bed. One night he was studying by a large candle since the light bulb in his room had burned out. He fell asleep, and the dog knocked over the table with the candle on it to get at the cookies.

The candle landed under my oldest son's bed and started his mattress on fire. He remembers feeling nice and toasty in bed (for a change) since his bedroom was not heated. What woke him up I don't know, but thankfully, he awoke. He remembers opening one eye and looking at the flames and smoke coming from under his bed. He tried jumping out of bed, but some of the mattress was stuck to him. He finally pulled free of the mattress.

He woke up his brother, and they grabbed some Jolly Good soda and tried to put out the fire. Their dad thought they were fighting upstairs and so did not pay any attention to them. When the soda didn't work, they decided to stuff the mattress out the window. They broke the window and tried to shove the mattress out, but it got stuck. My oldest burned his arms in the process. Their dad finally decided to see what was going on. He went upstairs, saw the mattress burning, and helped them get it out the window. They then called the fire department.

The fire was put out, and the boys were all right. My oldest son said that the point of the story is to have no lit candles in the bedroom when sleeping.

My one worry was removed; God had kept my boys safe. Why did the fire happen? Was it just a coincidence? I don't know. My boys both got renovated bedrooms out of this. I should have been there. Maybe they would have been safe and taken care of. Not being there was a hell in itself.

"Have patience, My child."

CHAPTER 23

The Gift

_____

If I were the minister, I would have had many questions. If someone just came out of the blue and told me about two dreams they had had about me, what would I do? I think I would be very skeptical. "Why me?" would be the first question. Then, does God send someone only to me? Is there anyone else this has happened to recently? Do I want to talk to another person? Does this happen in this day and age? What have I learned from all my reading about this?

Questions, questions, and more questions ...

Would I dismiss it as crazy or think about it a lot? Remember, I was asked if I were an angel!

The minister and I had some things in common. We were both divorced, the same age, and from Wisconsin. But we were not alike in lifestyle.

I had no idea why I was chosen to receive these dreams and hear these voices. I sure was not praying for this to happen. I had all these questions:

Why did I have to leave everything to deliver this message?

Why pick someone from over one thousand miles away?

What was the minister praying for in 1990?

Was I doing any of this right?

Why did God tell me to have patience with the minister?

I figured only the minister knew why the Holy Spirit picked him and what in his life needed to be worked on before he could be fully used by God. I, on the other hand, asked what in my life needed to be worked on. I am the type of person who needs to have everything in order and a direction. I was in limbo. Only God and the Holy Spirit knew. I was waiting and clueless. In what direction was God sending me?

I was trying to be obedient and not go back on my promise. I hated with a passion leaving my children and my life, but I still kept my word.

God was still teaching me patience, saying, "Have patience, My child." I repented of all my sins, and believe me, the Holy Spirit brought all of them to mind through Romans 7. I knew I was forgiven. In Romans 8, I received my salvation through God's grace by believing that Jesus Christ died for all of my sins and that His blood covers me. Not knowing what I was looking for, God in His gracious mercy saved me.

I now know why the Holy Spirit commanded me to read Romans. In the book *The Essential Bible Companion*, John H. Walton, Mark L. Strauss, and Ted Cooper, Jr. state that the central theme in Romans 6–8 is the righteousness of God. That all people are sinful and stand condemned before a righteous and perfect God. It is only through the sacrificial death of Christ on the cross that people can be made right with God. On the basis of Christ's payment for sin, God "justifies," or declares righteous, those who have faith in him.

Salvation is the best gift in the world. It is everlasting.

CHAPTER 24

Pure Evil

September 1992 was a pretty quiet month. I was sick for a week, probably from overworking and overstudying.

On October 4, I spoke with the minister about being a good Christian. What did it entail? I was trying to keep some type of rapport or interaction with him. I had only been telling him what was going on in my life as far as the dreams and the voices. I did not know how else to keep the lines of communication open.

It was all still very new to me. I did not have a lifetime of these experiences to fall back on. I also did not have anyone to talk to who had anything remotely similar happen to them. It had happened in the Old and New Testaments, but all those people are in heaven. I could only trust that I was doing it right and that God would correct me if I were wrong.

I was still going out with my friends and living a normal life. Then on October 10, I went to the movies with the woman who was infatuated with the minister. Since I did not have that type of relationship with him, I figured we could hang out together. But maybe not.

It was the most unsettling time. What I felt emanating from her was absolutely evil. It was so pronounced I thought everyone could feel it. Why did she seem jealous of me? I never knew that jealousy could conjure up such hatred. Besides, I was not dating the minister!

This scared me. Nothing has ever scared me like this. I could not wait to get out of there and go home. I never saw her again.

I was thankful for the intuition God had given me. It reminded me of my second dream of the distorted and mean faces of women coming out of the darkness. I was peaceful because Jesus was protecting me.

Then on October 12, I was standing at the kitchen counter making supper for myself. I was peeling potatoes to go along with a hamburger patty and broccoli. I can still picture that scene in my mind after all these years.

Suddenly, behind me and on both sides I was surrounded by pure evil. It was so strong; I was scared to move or to look around me. Nothing touched me, but whatever was there was evil. I didn't see anything. It was so unexpected. What to do? I was in a panic. I could have called the minister, but what if he wasn't there? I thought of all the people I could call, but I would have had to move to get to the phone.

Then, as a last resort, I prayed to Jesus, and as instantly as it had come, it vanished. Trembling, I sat down. I thought I was done with all of this. The dreams and voices I had were peaceful, but this was the exact opposite. Was this supposed to scare me? Why? Since I had no clue what I was doing in the first place or where this was going, it didn't make any sense. *Nothing* made any sense.

Why did God let this happen? The presence didn't hurt me or touch me; it was just there. I figured that the thing went away when I prayed to Jesus, which was all I needed to learn!

I had first sensed evil in the woman I went to the movies with and then the evil in my home. I had never thought of evil in the purest sense before. This was frightening. I was so tired and exhausted. I wanted this all to end and just get on with my life, whatever that was to be.

When you stop and think about how God, the Holy Spirit, and Jesus can pop in and out of your life, mine seems more dramatic than most, even incomprehensible. When you read the Bible, you are aware that people do hear God, the Holy Spirit, or Jesus's voice, but in their mind when awake or asleep. People do have dreams from God for specific purposes. Sometimes God reveals fantastic visions to some. So why was I having so much trouble accepting what was happening to me? The world says this does not happen in this day and age. But I say, "Yes, it does."

CHAPTER 25

Unexpected Third Dream

On October 16, I had a third dream. Again, it was a dream with two parts. Believe me, I was not praying or wishing for any of this.

In the first part of the dream, I was standing fully clothed next to a couch. The couch was long with no back. With the exception of one end, the rest was open. I looked down, and on the couch was a naked woman, knees raised and spread apart. I remember thinking that this looked disgusting and wondering why I was standing next to her. I did not recognize her and no one came to mind. I was still peaceful, though, and was not afraid to look at her. It's just that her pose was improper and vulgar.

Then came part two. I was looking up at the blue sky, and it was very peaceful. Then suddenly a perfect circle appeared, like someone had pulled apart the sky. Inside the circle was black, and then lightning bolts flashed from the dark opening. Many lightning bolts flashed, but none came near me. The lightning was impressive and magnificent.

Then I awoke, but I could still see the lightning on the inside of my eyelids. It was like looking at lightning during a storm and then shutting your eyes.

This is the second time a perfect circle had appeared. First, the minister saw the perfect circle with the colors of the rainbow inside it and now in my dream I saw a perfect circle with lightning coming from it. Why a perfect circle?

I remember sitting up and wondering what this was all about. It was truly beyond comprehension. I could not deal with this anymore. I could have pondered why I had had another dream, but I was so tired and wanted to go back to sleep. I would deal with this dream in the morning.

The next day, I called the minister. When we met, I told him about the dream. I do not know what he was supposed to do. I was hoping he would give me a hint or its meaning. I should have known that the interpretation would be made known to me when the time was right.

He suggested maybe it was about the woman I went to the movies with. It could have been, really stretching the interpretation, with the woman symbolizing nonbelievers and the second part the wrath of God on the nonbelievers.

Was this for the minister, or was it for me? Was it narrow in scope for only a few people? Was it encompassing the whole church? I truly needed discernment.

I prayed and started to look up Scripture in the Bible. I did not know what else to do. I had received the dream, so I was supposed to do something with it. Why was this dream given to me? Could not the minister have gotten this dream? I believed it was not for the minister, only for me. I was hoping God would send someone to interpret the dream, like Joseph did for Pharaoh.

Following are the Scriptures I came up with:

First, I looked up "woman, naked, on the couch." Since it looked disgusting to me instead of a woman in labor, I am going with a prostitute or whore. It was a very provocative pose. There are only a few mentions of a prostitute or whore in the Bible. The mention of prostitute is in Leviticus 19:29.

The Old Testament talks about not getting mixed up with a whore and not becoming one. The mention of a whore in the New Testament is in the book of Revelation. But neither Scripture was like my dream. I had no desire to become a whore or prostitute, nor did I know any. God would not give me a dream about something that was already in the Bible. It had to be more personal, something for me alone.

Next I looked up "lightning" in the Bible. There were numerous examples of lightning from Zechariah through Matthew and Luke and finally Revelation. Lightning was used to symbolize the coming of the Son of God. Lightning also comes from the throne of God to punish sinners. Was God telling me that Jesus was coming back in my lifetime? The Scripture says that no one knows. But I did not have a vision of the throne of God. The lightning could have come from God's throne; I just didn't see a throne or God.

The final thing I looked up in the Bible was "wrath of God." There are many verses in the New Testament regarding this. John 3:36, Romans 1:18, and Romans 2:5 come to mind.

The verses go on and on. How do they pertain to the dream I had? Did the dream pertain to me, someone else, believers, or the non-churched? Now I was getting more than a little stressed. I had no idea what to do.

I was really tired of dealing with everything. Finally, I made a mature move: I left this church on October 30, 1992, and went back to my previous church. It was a needed break. I was tired of thinking about any of this. I really did not know how to deal with these dreams and figured the minister could fend for himself. I needed some neutral space to unwind and not think about any of this.

However, I did not find the expected peace at my previous church either.

CHAPTER 26

Dream Fulfilled

On November 9, while sleeping I heard a gentle, quiet voice say to me, "He will shelter you under the shadow of His wings, if you abide in Me." This was very reassuring, but what did "abide" mean?

Off I went to study the meaning of "abide." From what I read, it means to have a relationship with Jesus wholeheartedly. That Jesus should be first in my life, and with the Holy Spirit's help, I should try to be more like Jesus every day. Do you know how hard that is to do? I have been trying the past twenty-three years and have fallen down more times than I have abided. I have been clinging to the hope that God is sheltering me, knowing how many times I had gotten it wrong.

I also was trying to figure out what I needed sheltering from.

At the time, I was working for a large brokerage firm when God did shelter me. The broker I was assigned brought back his previous assistant, and I was transferred to another broker, who had a horrible reputation. His previous assistants either asked to be moved to another broker or they quit after five minutes. My girlfriend had been his assistant before me, and she could not wait to be transferred. No one had anything good to say about him. I dreaded the move.

My first day as his assistant came. To my surprise, the broker had changed overnight into a kind, warmhearted, and wonderful person. No one could believe the change and wondered what I had done to him.

I knew God had somehow had a hand in it. The broker was so worried he was going to overwork me. I, on the other hand, was getting bored and not used to the pampering. I even wrote a nice letter to his superiors about what a great person he was to work for.

I was still attending my previous church when my friend who attended the church with the minister asked me to come back for a dinner on December 6. So I did. When I walked into the fellowship hall, I stopped next to the serving cart and looked out into the hall. To my surprise, the tables were arranged in the slanted position just like in my first dream and the minister was in the middle, surrounded by adults and children.

This was my confirmation. The dream I had had two years earlier in Wisconsin finally had come to pass. It was a dream from God.

The minister then disappeared into his office. I went to his office to see if he was okay. I don't know if he was glad that the dream came to pass or not, for that meant the other dreams would eventually happen. If I had not left the church and come back the night of the dinner, this would not have happened.

What I thought was a weakness, my getting so stressed out that I left the church, was actually God's plan all along. I have to remember that God is in charge and is all-knowing.

How could I know that this dream would take two years before it would come to pass? I had had the three dreams and heard the three voices in the span of three years. This was overwhelming, especially for someone who had never had anything like this happen before.

Why was each dream in two parts? Why only three, two-part dreams and three voices? Three is the number of the Trinity: God the Father, God the Son, and God the Holy Spirit. Each voice I heard was from one member of the Trinity. "Have patience, My child" was God the Father. "Romans six eight" was God the Holy Spirit, and "He will shelter you under the shadow of His wings, if you abide in Me" was God the Son. They were each different and distinctive, and I was given the knowledge of who was speaking. I probably will never know why I was so very, very blessed to hear each of them.

I have always had this fear of not doing something right, especially when the dreams involved someone else. Sometimes I am too rash and hasty or say the wrong thing, and I hope I don't mess up too much. I have to remember that I am not perfect by any stretch of the imagination. But God is perfect and will use my mistakes. He has given me the dreams and those were His voices I heard.

Mystery surrounds the things God chooses to do. Each encounter I have had with God, the Holy Spirit, and Jesus has been shrouded in some mystery, maybe to see if I will trust and obey Him. Most of it did not make sense to me at the time. I have to remember that God's thoughts and ways are perfect, and that my thoughts and ways are not.

God truly kept my eyes focused on Him. He taught me that the things of this world are nothing compared to Him.

God does not have to explain Himself to me or anyone else. I pray that He will always guide me in this life.

"Have patience, My child," He said.

CHAPTER 27

The Old Farmhouse

_____

The house of my sons' dad reminded me of where my father lived with his grandfather. I really had a hard time leaving them there. They were both as depressed as I was.

They never spoke to me about what the house was like. After the fire, their bedrooms were new, but the rest of the house was a mess. It should have been condemned.

In October, I came to stay with them while their father went hunting for a week. I was appalled when I walked in. This was where I had left my boys. Why did God let this happen? But I was so angry with myself, not God. I should have been there for my boys. This was no way to live. Then I was very angry with my ex-husband for letting the boys live this way. I wished I would have known how bad it was.

The first thing I did was clean the refrigerator. Only a half-dozen eggs were inside. I went grocery shopping and filled it with food.

Next I started cleaning. I scrubbed the entire kitchen, and then I started on the dining room, where the fire had left the walls black and the paint peeling off the ceiling. I scraped and washed and then painted the whole room.

The bathroom was worse. The window was broken, and the glass was still on the floor. There was a hole in the floor next to the toilet, and you could see the basement. Again, I scrubbed and cleaned and painted. I worked from early in the morning to late at night and slept with my clothes on.

I then cleaned their bedrooms and did over thirty-five loads of wash at the Laundromat.

I bought a new refrigerator and stocked it with food before I left. We did have some fun and a birthday party for my oldest son.

To move the boys the last year of high school was not a good idea. I was saving money to come home, not to move the boys with me. It killed me to leave them again.

Their uncle was more in their life than their father. I called him when I needed him to check on the boys to see how they were doing. My boys still have a great relationship with their uncle. He is a second father to them.

Both boys made it through high school and enlisted in the Marines. It was good for them to leave the area and experience something different. They learned discipline and saw a lot of the world.

David and me at the Marine Corps graduation ceremony.

Michael and me at the Marine Corps graduation ceremony.

After their time in the Marines, they both worked hard. David became an excellent licensed electrician, and Michael enrolled in college. After graduation, he became a sub-foreman for a large bridge construction company.

My boys had a simple life. I am so very proud of them and the wonderful men they have become. They both are great fathers, kind and loving. Sometimes God brings adversity into your life for many reasons, and it sometimes takes a lifetime to understand it.

I still have so many haunting questions. Why did I have to leave everything? What was the purpose? All I ever wanted was to raise my children and see them grow into young men. What would have happened if I had said no to God?

I still have this endless list of questions and no answers. My faith needs to increase a lot more to be able to cope with all that has happened.

PART 3

The Future and God's Plan

CHAPTER 28

The Future

The rest of December was uneventful, as was January and February of 1993. I had met a very nice man at a church outing, and we began to date. I was not looking for someone to date because I was planning on moving back home, but it was nice going out with someone. Still, I didn't want to get too involved.

How was I going to explain the dreams and voices to him? No guy is this understanding. But little did I know that God already had a hand in our relationship. Remember the night on August 8, 1992, when I sensed a presence in my place? Well …

I had invited the church group to my house for a get-together. The man I was dating came and stayed after to help me clean up. We put the folding chairs back in my bedroom closet when suddenly he said, "We have to talk."

He then told me about a dream he had had back in August when he was living in a different part of the state. In it, he was in a kitchen getting a drink of water and was looking through a rectangular hole in the wall to a dark room. Then he turned to his right and walked into a bedroom. He sat down on a bed and was looking at a maple dresser with an attached mirror with curves along the top. He then lay down on his side, facing the mirror. Not seeing anyone, he felt someone put his or her arm around him. He said he was scared to look behind him, as no one should have been there. He then fell asleep.

He said he only told me this because he recognized the kitchen and the opening to the dining room. But it only made sense when he was putting the chairs back in my bedroom and recognized the mirror on top of my dresser. He told me he was in a lot of turmoil the night of the dream. What are the odds?

I then told him my half of the story. God had arranged our meeting before we had even met! It took a lot of courage for him to tell me his dream. Anything is possible when God's hand is in the process. We continued to date.

Through March, I was still praying for the minister, hoping he would have a revelation and it would be over. I hoped to receive a time when the minister would figure this out. I heard in my mind that it would happen when "the lilies of the valley bloom," which is between May and June. But which May and June? Couldn't God have given me the exact date? We were now going toward the forty-year scenario.

All I know is that I did not have to be overly concerned about the minister. We did not have the best relationship through this process. Whenever I had knowledge that he was not working on his relationship with God, I would tell him. Mostly, I think he was taking his time to process everything. Maybe he didn't care at all about any of this. But I am always impatient. I needed to remember what God had first said to me, "Have patience, My child."

I had returned home for my youngest son's graduation from high school and stayed at a cottage by a lake that was surrounded by lily of the valley. I picked some and brought them back for the minister. I had someone place them on his desk with a note that had the following Scripture: "Be still and know that I am God" (Psalm 46:10). He called me, and we talked. I finally felt that I was done. He told me that the Scripture on the note was his father's favorite. Why I picked this particular Scripture I had no idea. The minister encouraged me and said I would grow more in my faith.

I told the minister about the dream because I had an overwhelming urge to do so, despite many people telling me not to. Remember, the first dream showing the fellowship hall with the minister standing in the middle surrounded by people had come to pass. Then I was standing in front of the minister when I looked into his eyes and was overcome by the most intense feelings. I had not yet seen this.

The second dream showed many ugly women's faces and the minister's spirit in turmoil. I had the minister go to church to keep him safe, where he received Scripture that was for him alone. In the second part of the dream, I saw the minister kneeling in front of a spiritual being. An angel? I might never know when this happens, but I am sure it will happen.

I found out that the minister had gone back to school and had received his doctorate of divinity and had remarried. I am so glad he is doing well. I know he will figure out what he is to give up so the glorious spirit I saw in the first dream can be unleashed.

"Have patience, My child" were the first words spoken to me and have always made me wait, somewhat. When I have been confronted with a problem or needed an answer, this is my first reaction. Things always seem to work out, usually never the way I expect them to.

I have a wonderful peace, knowing that God is in control and is sheltering me. Through this adventure, I have grown in my faith in Jesus Christ. Through His grace, God saved me and pointed me in a direction I never had in mind.

Chapter 29

God's Protection

The man I was dating asked me to go with him to his home state to pick up a van from the house of his ex-father-in-law. I was not sure I should do this, as it didn't seem proper. I prayed about this for a couple of weeks.

Then one night I received a dream. I was sitting in a house next to a fireplace. There were chairs on either side of it. Across the way sat a woman on a sofa. She had a short haircut. On the other side of the room was a woman sitting in a chair and a man standing next to her. Past them was another room, but it was dark. I had no idea where this was.

I related this to the man I was dating, and to my surprise, he recognized the room. It was the living room of his ex-sister-in-law. The people in the room were his ex-sister-in-law, ex-father-in-law, and his mother. I assumed that this was God's way of saying it was okay to go with him to his hometown to get the van. The man also told me to try to sit in a different place from what I had seen in the dream. I asked why, and he said that no matter what I do or where I try to sit, it would always turn out like my dream. To my surprise, I ended up in the same chair as in my dream.

How did he know this would happen? It seems he has always had premonitions since childhood when he was in turmoil about something. God reassured him in a dream.

We had a great time on the trip. We flew into the New Jersey airport and took the bus into New York City. I was excited to see the city. We had time to walk around, so we walked all over the city, seeing the sites and carrying our luggage.

An odd thing happened while we were walking. God was sheltering me again. My friend told me after we had boarded the train to Long Island that the whole time we were walking a glittering, dome-shaped, translucent object covered us. It was like looking through a billion tiny, glittering dots. The sun made it shimmer and shine. He could put his hand through it, but he never felt anything. He could see through it and knew we were safe if we stayed inside of it. It really made him anxious when I strayed outside of it. Only he could see it; I never sensed it at all. When he left for a moment to get the train tickets, it stayed around me, not him, and he felt very vulnerable. It left us when we boarded the train. He had no idea what it was, only that it kept us safe.

He purchased the van, and we drove it home. I will always remember the trip because he proposed to me, and I said yes. We had a lot to deal with. I had two sons, and he had a son and two daughters. His son and one of his daughters lived with him. His other daughter lived in Florida, and my boys lived in Wisconsin.

Another incident happened right before our wedding. When we were moving my things out of my condo, my fiancé had this horrible feeling that something evil was outside. It really scared him like nothing ever had before. He couldn't wait to leave. I, on the other hand, did not sense anything.

Why would he sense it and not me? What evil was there that I could not sense? This was like the same feeling I had inside my condo when the evil surrounded me. Why would this happen now? It did not make any sense whatsoever.

When he was on his way home, whatever was outside my condo was in the backseat of his van. He nervously drove for several blocks. It was late and dark, and there was no one on the road. Suddenly, a huge blinding flash lit up the inside of the van and the evil presence was gone. My fiancé became peaceful. He had no explanation for what had just happened.

We have been happily married now for twenty-two years. With all that was happening, I am surprised he still wanted to marry me. God must have given him the courage to do so.

CHAPTER 30

The Marriage

After we were married, we moved to another part of the state because of a job change and started going to a new church. At this church, the Holy Spirit called me to head up the Sunday school, as they needed a new director. You would have thought that I had learned to obey by now. But I thought of every excuse I could think of: I had never been in charge of a Sunday school. I was working full-time. We had kids. I didn't have enough time, and so on. Well, they hired someone else, and I was thankful I did not have to do it. However, the person they hired did not do anything to organize or order material. Then after a month, she left the church.

During that time, the Holy Spirit was really working on my conscience. I felt so bad that when the person left, I immediately volunteered for the job. What was I supposed to do now? I did not have a clue. But it was amazing what the Holy Spirit did.

I had all these wonderful ideas. I organized everything, which I am pretty good at. I literally had more ideas than I had time for. I was blessed with wonderful teachers and helpers. We started to do puppets for Vacation Bible School. It was in the evenings for five days with a meal for the whole family. We were led to create wonderful scenery. My husband designed and built the sets, and I painted and decorated them. We have been doing this for twenty-one years. So many children and adults have been touched during Vacation Bible School.

I also started a library because our church did not have one. I have always remembered my joy when I was studying. If I needed to study, maybe someone else would also be led to study, and the books would be available. I did not want anyone to go to another church for information like I had to.

We visited our previous church from time to time. The minister was always cordial but wary.

Situations always seem to present themselves to me. One day I decided to stop at a grocery store where I never shopped. I met up with a lady from our church, and we started talking about church, kids, and life in general. She told me that the mobile home she and her family lived in was leaking. It was so bad that mold was forming and the kids were getting ill. They are a wonderful family, very active in the church, and had just started a small business. We said good-bye and went our separate ways.

Over the next several days, I could not get her story out of my mind. Surely there was something that could be done to help this family. I spoke with the minister at our new church. He suggested that I ask the family if I could relate their story to the congregation. I did, and they agreed. I really wanted the minister to speak, but he said I needed to do it. I hate to speak in front of people, but that Sunday, I got up in front of the congregation and told their story. I was hoping to raise enough money to fix the mobile home. To my surprise, we collected more money that Sunday than our church had ever collected. I then thought we could buy a better mobile home for the family. But do you think that was what God had in mind?

I found a better mobile home in another county for the exact amount of money we had collected, only to find that we could not move a used mobile home from one county to another. Roadblock!

When we got back, I told the minister. He just happened to be reading about a program where they could get a stick-built house on their property if they owned the property. The family did not own it, but her father did. To make a long story short, her father gifted them the property. A house was built, and the money we raised was the down payment. God gets the credit for their wonderful home instead of my answer, which was another used mobile home. It pays sometimes to listen to others, to step out of our comfort zone, and let God take care of the rest.

Many years later, we moved to another church. To my surprise, they, too, needed a Sunday school director. So of course, I volunteered. My husband and I again did some wonderful scenery for Vacation Bible School, and I started writing the scripts for the puppet shows. It was such a joy to see the children enjoying the puppets and the scenery. The adults came every year just to see the scenery. Most of our children and grandchildren have started out as puppeteers and have grown to be fine adults.

Puppet scenery of a twenty-six-foot steam engine train
that my husband designed and built and I painted.

My husband designed and built a twenty-six-foot steam engine train as a puppet set for one of our Vacation Bible Schools. He was having trouble figuring out what to use as the large tube for the engine (See picture of train—tube). One day, he felt the urge to go to a specific intersection near his work, but he had never driven in that direction. On the side of the road was a truck and trailer, and in the trailer was a large tube. He asked the man next to the truck where he got the tube, and the man said he had purchased it from a company four hours away. The man asked why my husband needed it, and he told him it was for puppet scenery for Vacation Bible School. The man said my husband could have the tube since it was for Vacation Bible School. The tube happened to be the perfect size in diameter and the right length. It was a good thing that my husband listened to the urging and took a chance.

I had one more dream that was not related to the minister. I was working at Merrill Lynch at the time, and trying to save money for retirement. In the dream, I saw the stock market go up for a few days and then crash. I was never that obsessive about the stock market. I tried to plan and watch for good growth stocks. Over the next few days, I watched the stock market, and sure enough, it went up. Considering the dreams I had had before, I decided to act upon this recent one and sold everything we had at the market high. Several days later, the market crashed. Since then, I have been more prudent with our money.

Why God gave me the dream about the stock market I have no idea. But I am very grateful that we did not lose everything. I have never had another dream about the stock market.

CHAPTER 31

The Lesson

After seventeen years, my husband and I retired, and I finally returned to my home state. We built a house that my husband designed in a town between my boys. My son David was the general on the construction of the house. He did the electrical installation and hired the subcontractors, and Michael, my youngest son, did the painting and inside trim work. They both did the concrete work, and David did the landscaping. They did a wonderful job on the house and yard. They both are very talented and can do just about anything. They worked on the house in their off-time from work.

I am back with my boys, who are now married with children of their own. I left some wonderful memories, but have many more to make.

Before we retired, our church said prayers for a specific church in the new small town we were moving to states away. Our church had never prayed for a specific church before, except during Hurricane Katrina. We went to the new church and met the minister. During our conversation, he mentioned that they needed a Sunday school director. Again, what are the odds? Every church I have gone to since my spiritual adventure needed a Sunday school director. Of course, I volunteered.

What have I learned from this experience? God's time is definitely not my time. I would have liked to have a much shorter timeframe. Looking back on my experiences, I can see how all this weaved together. God does such a truly wonderful job if we let Him.

I never asked or wanted the dreams and voices, but God chose me for some unknown reason. That might be one of the several questions I will ask God when I die and go to be with Him.

There are no coincidences in God's plan. I never wanted to step out of my comfort zone. I am actually a very shy person. Yet against all odds, I left everything and told a minister about a dream. Everyone in my family thought I was odd when they found out about my experiences. I have had to overcome what people think about me. I had to do what seemed out of step with the world. And I received a wonderful gift from God in return: salvation! Everything else pales in comparison.

I never dreamed I would write this story and publish it. I am not a writer. I have been led to write this story. Why, I don't know. But I will wait patiently for the results.

One of the most important lessons is to be patient, no matter the circumstances. Our life has not been easy by any stretch of the imagination. We seemed to have more complicated situations than most. I know that God has His hand in everything that goes on in my life as well as everyone's on this planet. If God knows what is going on in my life and my family, I need to trust Him and be willing to do my best.

Sometimes I am caught off-guard and blow it. But I have learned that I do not have to be perfect. I grew up in a home where I felt I needed to be perfect for my parents to love me. But looking for that perfection took my focus off my relationship with Jesus. God wants us to be content with what we have and with who we are. We need to do what we have been called to do.

I have learned a lot by writing my story. I had to look at what had happened and what is still to happen. I had to write about all my flaws and mistakes. That is not easy to do.

Why the long span of time between when the dreams occurred and when they actually happen? The first part has happened, and the second part still has to occur. I pray all the time for clarification and study and search for answers.

God told me, "Have patience, My child" and showed me what would happen to the minister. Will the minister finally listen and be contented and full of joy? If so, when will this happen? Anything is possible. It is all in God's hands.

I still cannot fathom all that has happened. Why were the dreams so dramatic? Why me? Why this one minister? What does God see in us that warrants all this attention?

CHAPTER 32

My Mother

Since I lived with my grandmother until I graduated from high school and went away to college, I had a close relationship with my mother. My mother was caring and loving, strict but fair. We did many things as a family—picnics in summer at our favorite park, vacations all over the country, and just plain family time.

My mother's father was cold. He never hugged her or said he loved her. My mother reverted to that same coldness at times throughout my life. If she thought I was not being her ideal daughter, times got tough. I had a hard time living up to her ideals. It was the same for my sister. Neither one of us could live up to her perfect ideal child.

I finally decided it was okay to be myself. I could not fit into someone else's mold. God made me perfect in His eyes. But my sister has not yet figured this out. At every chance, she still tries to be the perfect daughter for my mother.

My husband and I visited my mother as often as we could. I always felt uneasy. There were no pictures of my family or me in the house. I would bring pictures of her grandchildren and great-grandchildren, but they would always seem to disappear. Her home was only full of pictures of my sister and her family.

My mother never asked me about my family, so we never talked about them when we visited. The more this happened, the more I withdrew and only talked about the weather. It was like none of us existed. Believe me, I was hurt and so were my children. I tried, but it did not do any good to address this with my mother.

When my mother went into the hospital, she called and wanted me to drive down to Florida, twenty-five hours away from Wisconsin. Our daughter who lives in Florida was having surgery the next week, and we had planned to go down to take care of our two grandchildren. Our son-in-law had died from cancer six months earlier.

I told my mother we would come down early to see her before our daughter's surgery. Since I had to do all the driving, it was going to take two days to get there.

I called her twice a day to check on her. While we were driving to Florida, she went into rehab and was doing great. Just before we reached our daughter's house, I called and was informed that my mother was in the emergency room of some hospital. My sister, who lives next door to my mother, was with her but never called. No one would tell me what hospital she went to. After calling every hospital in the area, I finally found her, but someone had told the nurses not to talk to me, and I could not prove over the phone that I was her daughter. I finally got ahold of my mother. When I asked her if she had told them not to talk to me, she said she hadn't.

I hated to think it was my sister. Trust was lost. My mother then said they were moving her to hospice.

When we got there the next day, my mother was mostly nonresponsive. I sat and held her hand. I don't know if she knew I was there or not. I did not address any of the hurtful things my sister said or did. I was there for my mother. My sister monopolized her the whole time, and I was alone with my mother for five minutes. During that time, I was finally able to say my good-byes.

It has taken me awhile to forgive my sister. But time seems to dull the pain. My sister did a wonderful job taking care of her. She was her best friend and lived in a condo on the same floor as our mother.

I do not have to do anything; God will take care of it. God showed me long before this happened to trust Him. I am only human. When I think about it, the hurts still wells up. It will always be in my memory. God is sheltering me from anything that is not good in this world.

CHAPTER 33

The Darkness

I could not figure out the second part of the last dream. It was very dramatic.

I always thought it was God's wrath. Not that it made sense; lightning usually means the coming of Jesus or the throne room of God. Since I didn't see the throne room or know when Jesus is coming, nothing made sense.

My husband is my rock and always tells me that when the time is right, I will understand the meaning. I needed to quit thinking so much about it. The trouble is that I was driven to write this story.

I actually stopped writing after I spoke with the minister in the dream in April 2011. I could not deal with all that emotion again. God had given me eighteen years where I never gave any of this a thought.

My husband and I had just finished Vacation Bible School when we both caught the flu. For two weeks, we felt under the weather. I slowly got better, but my husband didn't. He was having trouble breathing and had pressure in his intestines.

Our grandchildren from Florida came to stay for two weeks and wanted to have a good time. My husband seemed to get better and then would become worse. He finally went to the doctor. When he came home, he said I needed to drive him to the emergency room, as the doctor said he was having a heart attack. He was scared, and so was I.

We dropped off the grandchildren with my son and went straight to the emergency room. The doctor said he had fluid in his lungs, and they needed to get it out of his system. We laughed and cried, and I stayed close to him. They put an IV in his arm with a sedative, and he went out. The doctors then put a pump in his artery to help relieve the stress on his heart. I sat and waited while they did this and prayed. All this happened so suddenly that it was hard to take it all in.

My husband was moved to ICU. The doctors told me that his arteries were blocked. They talked about open-heart surgery, but my husband was not strong enough to have it done. They finally decided to put stents in the arteries to open the flow to the heart. However, that procedure is really hard on the kidneys, and they hoped he would make it through the surgery.

This was the second worst time of our lives. I cried constantly and prayed with every fiber of my being. God promises that the prayers of a righteous person will be answered and that prayer can move mountains. My faith is so strong, but I am still human. Doubts crept in, and I couldn't stop them. It is always darkest before the dawn, but sometimes it takes a lot of time before the dawn comes.

My friends came to stay with me through the surgery. Then the doctor came to say it went well. I was so relieved. But they still needed to put stents in the third and smallest artery.

On September 24, 2012, we had a setback and more darkness and dread. My husband started bleeding in his stomach, and his kidney functions were deteriorating. I hated seeing such a strong and caring man reduced to helplessness. I wished it were me instead. It was hard to hold back the tears.

Our oldest daughter was there and a blessing, as were our grandchildren who had come up for a vacation. We all sat at the hospital. At least I was not alone.

I prayed for healing, for the bleeding to stop, and his kidney function to improve. "God, please save him and improve his health," I said.

I looked back to my third vision, when I saw the lightning coming from the perfect black circle. I always thought it was God's wrath, but now I saw it was also His almighty and holy power, His presence, and His control. I felt peaceful when I saw that vision. There was no fear.

I have seen God in so many things: in His dreams to me, His beauty and majesty, and His overwhelming love, kindness, and joy. God's essence is so overwhelming that it is unbearable. The voice of God was so kind and loving, and when His peace descended upon me, it was overwhelming and indescribable. "Have patience, My child" was comforting, especially to one who has never had any patience.

I still do not know what I am having patience for. But I will wait until it is made known to me. This is the valley you don't want to go through. Why, why, why? Sometimes it is hard to keep your faith as strong as you need, as the unknown is always scary. Some days are better than most.

My husband's bleeding did not stop and his intestines were deteriorating. The doctors had a dire prognosis, telling me that if we were Catholic, we should administer the last rites. However, the doctors did offer another solution: surgery to remove the dying intestines, which would give him a 10 percent chance of survival.

Hell, I was tired. I spoke with our daughter, and we decided that 10 percent was better than zero. I said good-bye to my husband, and our daughter hugged me and said, "It will be okay." She then said, "It will be okay" again with more emphasis, adding, "I know."

Before they took my husband to surgery, they placed a green oxygen tank on his bed. Would this be the last time I would see him alive? I hoped not. Our daughter told me she had a dream where she saw a green oxygen tank on a bed with me standing next to it. She said she was very peaceful. That at least told me we had made the right decision. God was still sheltering and comforting me in a way that was unexpected.

I called both of my sons and asked them to come for moral support just in case the worst happened. Both came. I needed their hugs, just in case. It was nice having the kids and grandkids around. Our minister also came and stayed with us. We had a nice conversation; mostly I talked because I was nervous. I wanted his thoughts on lightning in the Bible. He had no suggestions other than what I knew from studying.

The doctor finally came out and said that the surgery had gone well, but it would be touch and go for the next few days. If our daughter and I had not made the decision, my husband would have died. God in His gracious mercy kept him safe during the surgery.

Our daughter took the kids to our house, and I slept in the conference room of the hospital. The summer was dry; we were in a drought, no rain at all. But that night, as I lay in the conference room looking out the large wall of windows, a sudden storm rolled in, the first storm in many, many months. As I was praying, a bolt of lightning flashed into my eyes. This brought back the second part of my last vision, God's power and majesty.

My husband improved the rest of the week with only minor setbacks. To keep him calm, the doctors put him in an induced coma for three weeks. Everything seemed to click along. The doctors were amazed at how well he was doing.

When they brought him out of the coma, he had ICU delirium, which was scary. He would see things that were not there, like a herd of cattle running through the room. It took five days for the medication to work out of his system, and that seemed worse than his surgery. I was never as happy as when he finally knew who I was. Just hearing him say that I was his wife was more than words can describe.

It took another week for him to learn to walk and regain his strength. Finally, he was able to go home. It was so nice being home at last. I had extra time to tend to the house, lawn, and garden, and my canning and freezing fruits and vegetables increased because we were at home all the time. Seeing the freezers full and the jars of beautiful fruits, salsa, pasta sauce, pickles, and jellies sitting on the shelves brought such satisfaction. The colors in the jars were fantastic: red, green, purple, and yellow. They gave me peace.

When we returned to the hospital for the last surgery, two more stents were inserted. I was peaceful during it, for I had prayed a lot and then left it up to God. I figured God had pulled my husband through the first two surgeries; He would get him through this one.

Everything went well.

My husband loves trains. His dad worked his whole life for the Pennsylvania Railroad in Sunnyside Yard, Long Island, New York. My husband has an HO train set up in our basement. When we went to a railroad museum in Wisconsin, to my husband's surprise, it had a Pennsylvania Railroad GG-1 Electric Locomotive. I took many pictures to decorate his train room. It was a great outing after living at the hospital for four months.

John with the Pennsylvania Railroad GG-1 Electric Locomotive.

Meanwhile, I prayed about being the Sunday school director and doing Vacation Bible School. I was really tired. I did not have the spark I usually did. But my heart was still with the children. So I needed to stop, think, and pray. Was I finally done with everything? I didn't know. It was hard for me to let go of things and to trust others.

The funny thing is that God always has a plan. One of my Sunday school teachers told me she wanted to do Vacation Bible School. God had brought someone who was excited to do it, and I had peace that she would. I thank God that he brought someone to take over. I was able to mentor her and that was enough. I was not a Sunday school director or doing Vacation Bible School anymore.

CHAPTER 34

Faith and More Surgeries

My husband was well enough and wanted to do the Christmas program for church. We already had all the scenery and I made all the costumes, so we did a traditional program. But during the program, he had severe pains in his intestines. He had an ostomy bag from the previous intestinal surgery, which was to be reversed the next year.

After the program, I rushed him to the hospital. They said he had a large kidney stone, and the doctors wanted to operate and break it up. We said okay.

The surgery went well, but we found out that he had had a stroke during the surgery and could not stand up. He had vertigo and the hiccups twenty-four hours a day. For three days they did physical therapy with him, but there was not much improvement. They suggested a month in a rehab facility, as he still had the hiccups.

I had stayed with him constantly throughout all his surgeries, so I was not about to let him out of my sight. He needed my comfort and care. God still works wonders.

My husband was moved to another hospital with a wing for intense therapy, but he was in a room with two other patients. How was I going to take care of him for a month by sleeping in a chair the whole time? That must be why he had the hiccups. They couldn't put him in a room with other patients, for they would get no rest. So they put us in the only private room they had for the entire time he was there. I had a bed to sleep in and could be with him. After ten days, the hiccups left, and he worked hard with the therapists on walking. After a month, he walked out of the hospital.

We met so many wonderful people during this time. The nurses and patients became friends. I am thankful for the wonderful care the nurses gave my husband.

At home again, my husband was getting better every day. His goal was to have the surgery to reverse the ostomy bag. The heart doctor still needed to put in more stents to keep his arteries open. That surgery went well with no side effects. But that meant we had to wait another year to have the ostomy reversed. Well, several kidneys stones later, my husband opted for no surgery. The stones passed, and we got closer to the one-year timeframe.

It was finally time to reverse the ostomy. My husband had a stress test and seemed to pass it, but the doctor still wanted to do a heart catherization and check on one area. After the procedure, the doctor came in with the good news. "You need open heart surgery." We were in shock and cried.

Two days later, we had an appointment with the surgeon, who went through the procedure and all the risks. I tried to hold back my tears.

The surgery was scheduled for the following Monday. I called our oldest daughter and flew her up to be with her dad and me. My husband had been through so much. We didn't need this. We needed a break. *I* needed a break.

The day of the surgery, I kissed my husband, hoping it wasn't for the last time. It was a five- to six-hour surgery, so our daughter and I settled in for the long wait. I felt so very peaceful, and so did she. That peace stayed with us the whole time he was in surgery.

Finally, the surgeon came out and said it went very well. He had replaced four arteries and said my husband would be in ICU for a few days.

Our daughter and I made ourselves at home in the lobby for the night. After trying to sleep in chairs, we decided to take the cushions and head for the floor of the conference room. It was a long night on the floor, but we did get some rest.

Every day my husband got better, and by the end of the week, he was up and walking out of the hospital. It was amazing. After having his chest split open, he had no pain at all.

And what a miracle: no stroke!

Two months later, he had surgery to reverse the ostomy bag, which went well. But two days later, he had another stroke. It was not as bad as the first one, and he went home after one week. It took over a year to get him more regulated and functioning well, but he made it.

My husband has a strong faith, but more importantly, he tackles every problem with a smile and with humor. We made so many friends at the hospital. The nurses and aides were absolutely amazing, and the doctors were brilliant.

But it was God who was in control of everything. Someday we will see why all this had to happen and why we met so many people and shared our story. It gave hope to some and laughter to others, and many people shared their stories with us. Maybe sharing our amazing journey helped others. And others sharing their journey with us helped our bond grow stronger.

I had always prayed that my mother would get some understanding about the dreams I had received. One day, she said she had had a dream. She saw my father, who had passed away several years earlier, standing in the living room. He had a smile on his face and was holding a book. So, Dad, this book is for you!

I still have not received the information on the last dream. But as God said, "Have patience, My child."

God's almighty power

The rest of our story has yet to come, with God's blessing.

Printed in the United States
By Bookmasters